MERCURIAL

FASA CORPORATION

•

1989

MARIA MERCURIAL

Concept
Tom Dowd
Paul Hume

Design
Paul Hume

Editorial Staff
Senior Editor
Donna Ippolito
Editor
Jim Musser
Editorial Assistant
C. R. Green
Research Assistant
Kent Stolt

Production Staff
Production Manager
Sam Lewis
Art Director
Dana Knutson
Cover Design
Jeff Laubenstein
Illustration
Joel Biske
Jim Nelson
Tim Bradstreet
Rick Harris
Barry Crain
Earl Geier
Tammy Daniel
Maps
Joel Biske
Layout
Tara Gallagher

Published by
FASA Corporation
P.O. Box 6930
Chicago, IL 60680

TABLE OF CONTENTS

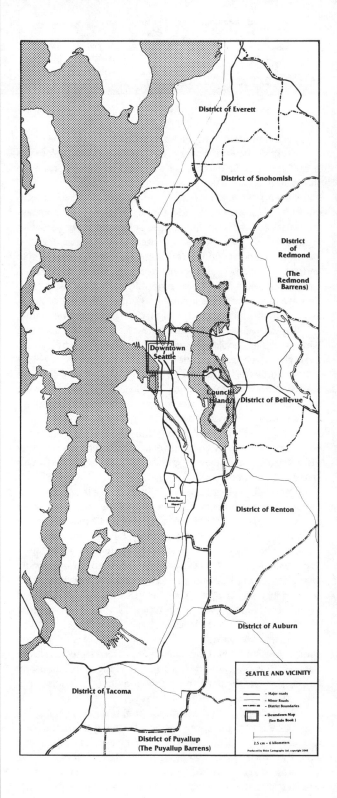

District of Everett

District of Snohomish

District of Redmond

(The Redmond Barrens)

Downtown Seattle

Council Islands / District of Bellevue

District of Renton

District of Auburn

District of Tacoma

District of Puyallup (The Puyallup Barrens)

SEATTLE AND VICINITY

- Major roads
- Minor Roads
- District Boundaries
- Downtown Map (See Rule Book)

2.5 cm = 6 kilometers

Produced by Blake Cartography Ltd. copyright 2048

OUT AFTER DARK: A Prologue

Just another night in the Sixth World.

Night's usually for working, but I wanted to relax before this latest bit of biz. Some runs are tougher than others and even shadows need a break.

On impulse, I gunned the Harley Scorpion into the fringes of the Puyallup Barrens, heading for the Underworld. Don't ask me what brought it on. Sometimes self-flagellation goes with my line of work. I honestly didn't remember that Maria Mercurial was playing Underworld 93 that night, not until I got to the club and saw her name flashing out over the packed streets in a rainbow of colors from the holographic marquee. I had a crazy impulse to spin the bike around and burn a path out of there, away from the coiling letters of light that spelled out her name.

The crowd was a wild mixture of street slime from the Barrens rubbing shoulders with corporate *shaikujin* from Bellevue, the high and the low of Seattle crammed into a grungy city block to pay court to the rocker queen. Security was heavy, with Lone Star cops keeping things cool. The line coiled back from the main entrance, writhing like a giant python with heartburn. Most of those who made it to the door got a thumbs-down from Newt, the oversized Troll who is the Underworld's arbiter of elegance. No one was going to get in tonight who wasn't either macroflash or outrageously grungy enough to please Newt's sense of the grotesque.

Of course, if you're a heavy politico, corp exec, media star, or occupy some other niche at the top of the food chain, then ordinary rules don't apply. I was carrying an ID that would get me past the gates of Heaven, assuming St. Peter knew what was good for him. The face on it was mine, though the rest of it was about as real as a politician's promise. I flashed it at the roadie who guarded the side entrance to the club, and was amused to see him instantly straighten up. The 100¥ bill wrapped around it probably helped. With some types, hard cash was a more enticing bribe than a credstick.

Underworld 93 was alive that night. Light blasted into my eyes as I walked down the ramp leading from street level. The dance floor was an amorphous beast, writhing with a thousand limbs, and the beat of the music red-lined my pulse into overdrive. On the stage, a nova was dancing.

Arms, legs, and face of mirror-bright metal, catching the searing beams of the spotlights and throwing them back in a dazzling cascade of color and light. That was the first thing you saw. Then the hair, flaring golden in the glare, surrounding her face like a solar corona around a silver moon. Only afterward did you register the athlete's firm torso, muscles ridged with exertion, the all-too-human core of this robotic finery. Maria Mercurial danced and while you watched her, nothing else mattered.

She was synth-linking the music, driving the banked-up sound machines with the impulses of muscle and nerve. Most kids who fancy themselves rockers just learn a few basic trigger patterns for their links, and let the programming of the control decks fill in the rest. Hearing and seeing Maria, you knew that every tone was driven by a highly trained movement, that the choreography of sound, body, and voice were all from the heart, as alive as children at play, as intimate as a lover's caress, as real as death.

The voice was uniquely hers, yet it was also that of every woman you've ever loved...or hated. One moment it spit in your face like a street killer high on Black Thunder. The next second it ripped out your heart like the cry of a starving child, or nailed you to the wall with a blazing spike of pure animal heat.

One of my oldest friends collects old rock and roll recordings the way some people collect jewels or antique cars. Maria's voice always reminded me of some from those days, when the juice still ran hot through the music. Grace Slick comes to mind, or Janis Joplin, who burned out like a comet that got too close to the sun.

When the set was over, the Underworld went berserk. Maria stood under a single, searing spot at the center of the stage, her chest and belly pumping in deep, gasping breaths. The metal limbs shimmered as rivulets of sweat poured down from the human flesh of shoulders and hips.

It was almost ten minutes before the demented crowd would let her go. I felt a crazy wave of hate flash through me at the way they screamed for more, when she'd already given more than human flesh, hers or theirs, should be able to stand. If she'd danced her life out on the stage and died for their pleasure, they'd still have shrieked their hunger.

This had begun as a night off, but when your karma says it's time to work, you work. So the Harley and I were ready, waiting in an alley by the stage door, when Maria ran the gauntlet of fans to her limo. The big Mitsubishi Nightsky, mirror-chromed like its mistress from hood to trunk, pulled into the dark streets, and I eased out in its wake, trailing along a block behind.

I was only a little surprised when the limo turned deeper into the Barrens, away from the lights of the city and into Seattle's own little heart of darkness. Sometimes, after a gig, Maria had to unwind. Her file made it clear how she would do it. I thumbed for a weapons check, and the Scorpion's console reassured me that it was ready for any little unpleasantness that the zone might send my way.

A block away from a razor-guy dive called The Armadillo, her car pulled over to the curb. Seeing that the driver had deployed his weaponry, I silently applauded his excellent good sense. The back door opened, and Maria stepped out. She was wearing a black street outfit, armorcloth set with silver splints, that looked like a fetishist's dream come true and would probably stop a magnum slug at close-range. Baroque glasses covered the upper half of her face with black lenses so opaque they had to be vision-augmenters. She'd have been blind otherwise. She said something to the limo driver, and walked into The Armadillo as the car pulled away. I parked the bike, told it to frag anybody who even looked at it sideways, and followed her in.

The joint was crammed with the wannabees, used-to-bees, and assorted killer-bees of the samurai scene. The vibes were a veritable oratorio of bad-ass. Maria was at the bar, constructing a margarita out of whatever toxic waste they sold under the alias of tequila. Several grimy-nasties approached her, offering dubious pleasures, and backed away when their best efforts didn't merit even a glance. Finally, a guy who might have been a Troll, except that Trolls rarely get so big or so ugly, locked target-acquisition on the lady. When his opening line got nowhere, he decided to drop the coy approach and grabbed her arm.

There was a liquid movement of black and silver, and then the ardent suitor sailed into a knot of onlookers. Maria stood with her back to the bar, her onyx-lensed shades catching faint reflections from the lights overhead. Ugly boy seemed stunned, which was understandable, then let out a roar as what happened sank into his consciousness. He charged forward. Why do these muscle jobs always charge when they run into someone who can take them? Doubtless a shrinker could find deep and mysterious tendencies in the pattern. It's almost like they're programmed for it: get thrown, stand up, roar and charge.

With an avoidance move so fine I expected the crowd to burst into applause, Maria took herself off the guy's line of attack. One silver hand slipped over his outstretched, clutching arm, the other looped up to grasp the back of his neck. She stepped aside, continuing the turn she had begun, and cartwheeled the goon over the bar into a pyramid of bottles. The destruction was awesome.

There is something about the sound of breaking glass in places like this. Within seconds, the bar turned into one, humongous brawl. I pistoned the heel of a hand into a snaggle-toothed face that got too close and followed a trail of flying bodies that marked the quicksilver lady's path to the door. Once outside, I scanned for a second before I heard the wrenching sound of someone being violently sick in a doorway down the block. Moving as silently as I knew how, I moved into position to check it out, and was rewarded with the sight of Maria vomiting against the stoop. I could also see two furtive figures in the shadows, inching closer and closer to the bent-over figure. The lone streetlight on the corner caught the gleam of steel in their hands.

I pulled my Viper. "Nothing personal, guys," I muttered, as the tiny red spot of the laser sight popped into being. The deadly needles *phutted* as they drilled into the thuggers' foreheads. Out of the corner of one eye, I could see the silver limousine turning the corner, come to retrieve its owner after her brief night out. Maria was sitting in the trash on the bottom step of the brownstone, hands over her face, crooning to herself in a quiet, steady voice. The elaborate shades lay shattered on the pavement, twisted out of shape as if a powerful, metal leg had stamped them again, and again, and again. Her personal demons had been laid to rest, at least for tonight, by the twin drugs of music and violence.

The chauffeur climbed out of the car, cradling a short, ugly shotgun under one arm. He bent over the rocking figure and spoke quietly. She looked up. I had my eyes turned up to deal

with the darkness, and under the ghostly light of the dim streetlamp, I could see her face plainly. I have never understood why the late and unlamented Reynaldo Texamachach had left the eyes unaltered when he had Maria's skin job done. Maybe there was something about the deep, brown, living eyes looking out of the silver mask of her face that did something for him. It always made me want to cry, or kill something.

I watched as the pair went back to the car. The driver handed Maria into the rear seat like she was royalty. Then he got into the front and burned rubber getting away from that little corner of Hell. Smart fellow.

I walked back to where I'd stashed the Harley, and kicked away the twitching body of a local with more greed than sense who had gotten too close to the electrically charged anti-theft plates. They retracted when I told the bike I was back. As I wheeled my way back to base, I nearly had to stop for a good puke myself.

Maria Mercurial. I'd studied her. Seen her make her art and found joy in it as I watched. With the access to her files that my masters at Aztechnology had given me, I knew her better than she knew herself. Now all I had to do was kill her. Some runs are tougher than others.

INTRODUCTION

Maria Mercurial is a roleplaying adventure set in the world of **Shadowrun.** The year is 2050. Advances in technology are astonishing, with humans able to blend with computers and travel through that netherworld of data known as the Matrix. Even more astonishing is the return of Magic. Elves, Dragons, Dwarfs, Orks, and Trolls have assumed their true forms, while megacorporations rather than superpowers rule much of the world. Magicians and Shamans wield another kind of awesome power. Moving among it all like whispers in the night are the shadowrunners. No one admits their existence, but no one else can do their secret work.

This story takes place in the streets and shadows of Seattle, now an urban sprawl encompassing some 1,600 square miles from Everett to Tacoma. Yet even this vast megaplex is but an enclave set amid even larger states ruled by Native American nations and other sovereign states of metahumans and Awakened Beings.

GAMEMASTERING NOTES

Except for certain items clearly marked as handouts for the players, the contents of this book are for the gamemaster's eyes only. To run the adventure, the gamemaster needs familiarity with the basic **Shadowrun** rules. For convenience of play, some character stats have already been factored to reflect enhancement or modification by certain gear or abilities. These are so noted.

Six is the optimum number of players for roleplaying **Maria Mercurial.** Any fewer and the players' team is likely to be overwhelmed. Any larger and the group could become so unwieldy that the pace of play begins to drag or totally bogs down. Experienced gamemasters are, however, the best judge of their own and their players' abilities when it comes to size of the group.

This adventure combines several approaches. Some encounters are planned and others remain open-ended. Hints for gamemastering the various situations are included with the individual sections describing the adventure.

The players are free to select their own characters, but the gamemaster should be aware of several types that will enhance the team's ability to roleplay **Maria Mercurial**. As the adventurers will encounter magical opposition, it would be handy if they have their own wizard among them. Also, the team will miss out on some useful clues unless they have a decker. Finally, this run includes a lot of combat, so the player characters should include some decent muscle.

HOW TO USE THIS BOOK

Aside from the basic **Shadowrun** rules, this book includes everything needed to play this adventure. For best results, the gamemaster will familiarize himself with the contents of the book before the start of play. The twists and turns of the plot are intended to take the players by surprise, *not* the gamemaster.

Though this booklet tries to cover all the likely—and even unlikely—things that can happen during the adventure, it is impossible to foresee everything. The gamemaster may find that sometimes it is a good idea to just let the unexpected lead where it will. Even if it does turn out that everyone gets killed, hey, they knew the job was dangerous when they took it. On the other hand, if the players do something truly clever to outsmart the bad guys and win the day, the gamemaster can keep them on their toes by wrapping things up with a big fight when the thwarted villains come back for revenge!

The **Plot Synopsis** is a fairly detailed summary of both the story background and the course the adventure is intended to follow. The interview with Maria Mercurial from *Rocker Stars* and the lyrics from her first hit record are presented as Player Handouts to help the gamemaster stimulate the players' interest in this adventure.

The Adventure begins with a section entitled **Getting Into It,** which offers suggestions for how to get the ball rolling and draw the characters into the adventure. Then follow a number of short sections describing each of the encounters that the players will face or are likely to face in the course of roleplaying **Maria Mercurial**. In those instances where the team might choose among several different options, each of those options is fully described as a separate section.

Most of the encounters begin with a text entitled **Tell It To Them Straight.** This is intended to be read, verbatim, to the shadowrunners. It describes where they are and what is happening to them as though they were there. Any special instructions to the gamemaster are printed in boldface type and signaled by the words "Gamemaster's Notes." In some cases, there are two or more possible texts given, and the gamemaster reads only the one appropriate to what has occurred earlier in the story line.

Next comes the information entitled **Behind The Scenes.** This is the real story, for only the gamemaster knows what is really going on at any given moment in an adventure. If there is a map needed to play this encounter, it is included in this section. Non-player character stats needed to roleplay the section are usually included here also. When a fight is likely, the gamemaster will also find hints on how the bad guys might handle themselves.

Finally, most sections include hints entitled **Debugging.** These notes could include suggestions for getting the story back on track if things go too far wrong at this point in the adventure. For example, most gamemasters will not want the characters to get too discouraged or killed off too easily. The gamemaster is, of course, always free to ignore these hints and let the chips fall where they may.

The **Cast Of Characters** section describes the three major NPCS—Maria, Max Foley, and Armando Hernandez—and gives their statistics. Stats and information on other important NPCs such as Sumiko Hotoda, Kyle Morgan, the Dragon Perianwyr, and Morgan's "Dragon Knights" are presented at the point where the character(s) shows up in the story.

Finally, there is a section called **Picking Up The Pieces,** which includes an epilogue, tips for assigning the karma, and news-net items for handout to the players, depending on the adventure's outcome.

PLOT SYNOPSIS

Maria Mercurial tangles up the shadowrunners in a nasty web of double-dealing and danger. They *think* their job is to protect rock star Maria Mercurial, who is being threatened by her former agent, Armando Hernandez. Hernandez is angry that Maria has canceled her contract with him and signed on with his arch-rival, Max Foley. Sounds like a straightforward bodyguard gig, right?

What nobody knows, not even Maria herself, is that until five years ago, she was bodyguard, secretary, and mistress to Reynaldo Texamachach, a senior exec at Aztechnology. He loaded her skull with sealed memory and bought her a major

DREAMCHIPS

In the year 2050, drug use has largely been replaced by the use of illegally modified simsense chips. Technically, they generate simsense signals at amplitudes that intensify the experience to the limits of tolerance, or beyond. Common names for these are dreamchips, Better-Than-Life (BTL), and brain-strain, among others. Users are dreamchippers, deckheads, ROM-burners, and so on.

Dreamchips can induce numerous pre-programmed fantasies, with direct stimulation of the pleasure centers of the brain. They are profoundly addictive psychologically, though there is no evidence of physical addiction. The typical chip is timed to prevent undue trauma to nerve cells, and usually designed to burn itself out after one play to keep addicts coming back for more. Dreamchips plug into a standard datajack.

The constant use of dreamchips is highly addictive. In addition, extended use results in cumulative damage to brain cells, making the addict less sensitive to the effect. Thus, users must obtain more frequent doses or increase the amplitude of the signal still further, thus increasing brain cell damage. This vicious cycle usually ends with the death of the user. Other effects can be nerve damage, memory loss, or psychotic episodes.

Chips are often modified to play continuously. Timers, self-erase features, and similar safeguards can be overcome by technically competent persons. On the street, such modified chips are known as dreamgates. They are usually one-way gates. Subjects hooked into a continuous high-amplitude simsense broadcast suffer death within a short time as autonomic systems break down under the high-energy brain stimulation. Death by this means, either as suicide or as murder by giving someone a "loaded" chip, is a staple in cheap adventure fiction.

Dreamchips can be custom-designed, attuned to an individual's neural structure and psychological profile. Such chips can be addictive after one exposure. Withdrawal from a custom chip is agonizing, and users often expose themselves to high dosages of standard dreamchips if cut off from a custom chip.

skin job, real cutting-edge, state-of-the-art cybertech. Texama-chach also addicted her to dreamchips. That is, BTLs (Better-Than-Life), illegal simsense chips. With Maria hooked on custom chips that only he could provide, Texamachach figured to keep her obedient to his every whim.

In 2045, during a trip to Seattle, Maria rebelled, killed Texamachach, and escaped into the Barrens. Still hooked on dreamchipping, she fed her habit by working as a prostitute. One night, a music promoter named Armando Hernandez heard her sing. So impressed was he that he got her out of the Barrens, put her into a clinic to kick the BTL habit, and then began to promote his discovery on the rocker circuit.

Ever since the agony of dreamchip withdrawal, Maria has almost no memory of her life before Hernandez found her and she goes through personality changes that are almost psychotic. Indeed, her personality shifts in and out of three personas, the Amazon, the Schoolmistress, and the Innocent. Lacking any recall of her former name or identity, the beautiful singer kept the handle that she had used as a "working girl" in the Barrens.

Almost immediately, Maria Mercurial rocketed to stardom. Her first single, "Who Weeps for the Children?" was number one on the charts for two months in 2048, before her second single "Take It To Mister," replaced it. When she released her second album, "Puta," in 2049, and followed that up with a 28-city tour that played to packed houses all the way, she became a true novastar.

With all this flash and fame, the Aztechnology corps knew Maria's whereabouts, but the risks of messing with such a big-name star outweighed any desire to avenge Texamachach. As someone once said, revenge don't show on the bottom line. Corporate shadowrunners got copies of Maria's records from the detox clinic that indicated she had lost her memory. Because she could no longer reveal anything damaging to Aztechnology, the corps had no reason to look for trouble. That, at least, was their policy until recently, when they learned that Maria held the key to a very sticky situation, indeed.

Perfekto Polymers is an Aztechnology subsidiary involved with plastics manufacturing. In 2045, Maria's boss, Texamachach, was sent to Seattle to deal with problems at a local Perfekto plant. It seems that the bright lad who was running the place had decided to cut costs by violating Seattle's dumping laws. Rather than pay for recycling industrial wastes or transporting them back to designated dump sites in the UCAS, far from the NAN territories, he had been secretly dumping the wastes into a large, underground tank.

As everyone knows, Seattle law comes down heavier on dumpers than it does on murderers. The Treaty of Denver is sudden death on industrial pollution in Native American Nation territory or areas bordering NAN turf. Of course, the Perfekto exec figured that no one would find out about his little scheme.

And no one did until the local cell of Greenwar, an eco-terrorist policlub, made a run on Perfekto Polymers' mainframe. Among other goodies, they came up with a secret report on the amount of nuyen the plant was saving because of the waste-dumping scam. Greenwar intended to release the data to the news-nets, which would surely have led to meganuyen fines and clean-up costs for Perfekto Polymers. Worse, if the neighboring NAN councils got hot enough about Perfekto's "poisoning the land," they could bring pressure to deprive the company

of its license to operate in the Seattle region. Besides the embarrassment to Aztechnology, all this publicity could have hosed up some delicate trade negotiations the megacorp was then conducting with the Seattle City Council.

Fortunately for Perfekto's bottom line, the drekheads in charge of Greenwar had the urge to gloat. They left a nasty note in the CEO's computer mailbox, telling him that they were going to stick it to the big, bad corp. In a panic, the head of Perfekto yelped for help from his bosses at Aztechnology, and they sent in Texamachach to fix things up.

Finding no tidy solution to the problem, Texamachach ordered a total cover-up. He closed down the plant, shattering the economy of the surrounding neighborhood and transforming the area into a hopeless slum almost overnight. The overly creative plant manager was dispatched back to Mexico City for a "special managerial briefing," but has never been heard from since. By strange coincidence, several night-shift technicians who had run the waste disposal system met fatal accidents. The local Greenwar cell was also wiped out by a strike force of Aztechnology shadowrunners.

All references to the waste disposal site were secretly purged from Perfekto's records. Texamachach, as usual, stored his final report in the sealed memory of his very private secretary, where it would be safe until they got back to corporate headquarters. This report contained the only record of the waste tank's whereabouts.

Unfortunately for Texamachach, his secretary chose that night to blow his brains all over his suite in the Aztechnology pyramid, then fled into the slums of the city. Though Maria has been carrying the secret data around in her head ever since, she is totally unaware of it.

Over the past year, a firm called New Horizons Development has been secretly acquiring property in the abandoned zone surrounding the former Perfekto Polymers plant. A neighboring area of the city is about to undergo major economic growth as part of another corporate expansion: office space, industrials, housing, the whole works. New Horizons, armed with inside information about this plan, intends to gain control of this slum real estate and renovate it for housing. When the price goes up, they will make out like bandits, selling condos to the suits working in the new offices and factories.

When New Horizons began clearing and construction last month, Perfekto Polymers got very nervous. If the construction crews accidentally breached the waste-disposal tank, the resulting spill could turn the area into a poison desert. Perfekto decided to notify New Horizons that millions of liters of hideously toxic industrial wastes were buried somewhere in their development. New Horizons stopped all construction.

Then Perfekto management got a report from their shadowrunners that scared the drek out of them. It seemed that New Horizons Development was, in fact, owned by the Shigeda-gumi, a powerful Seattle yakuza syndicate.

It was at about this time that New Horizons presented Perfekto Polymers with an ultimatum. Either tell them the location of the waste site and pay the cost of cleaning it up, or they would leak word to the media. With the media baying for Perfekto's blood, New Horizons would be able to sue, with a good chance of getting anything they asked for from the courts. In addition, New Horizons representatives suggested that certain elements of their upper management were calling for stronger measures. Obviously, the Shigeda were royally ticked off. People who irritate yakuza gangs have very short life spans.

Perfekto's management was in panic mode, and sent a frantic appeal to the higher-ups at Aztechnology. It was then that the mega-corp discovered that Texamachach had stored his only copy of the data in Maria's sealed memory before his untimely death at her hands. This sets the stage for the adventure to begin.

Aztechnology has flown a troubleshooting team to Seattle. Bossed by top corporate shadowrunner Kyle Morgan, the team's codename is "Dragon Knights." The Shigeda have assigned Sumiko Hotoda, one of their best mages, as liaison to the Aztechnology agents.

Morgan and Hotoda have devised a plan to kidnap Maria without implicating Aztechnology or the Shigeda-*gumi*. Instead, they intend to let her manager, Armando Hernandez, take the fall.

Meanwhile, Shigeda loan sharks are holding 500,000¥ worth of past-due notes from big-name talent agent Max Foley. Shigeda enforcers were about to close his account—permanently, when the top yaks realized that Foley is a long-time business rival of Armando Hernandez. This would fit perfectly into the plan. The Shigeda tell Foley that he will get control of Maria's career so that he can sign over part of her earnings to the gang syndicate to pay off his debt. He eagerly agrees to the Yakuza plan (as though he had any choice in the matter).

Hotoda arranges for Maria to see faked evidence linking Hernandez to the Shigeda's traffic in dreamchips. Horrified that someone she trusts is pushing BTL, which she now hates with a passion, Maria impulsively dumps Hernandez and signs on with Foley.

This sets the stage for part two of the bad guys' plan. Maria and Foley receive threats, apparently from Hernandez., warning that if Maria sticks with Foley, both her career and her life are in danger. Foley is panic-stricken, believing the threats are real and that his arrangement with the Shigeda is at risk. Sumiko Hotoda tells him that the Shigeda have done enough; it is up to him to deal with the situation. Foley decides to hire a team of shadowrunners to protect both Maria and his own butt. Of course, he also keeps Hotoda informed of the situation, and she, in turn, keeps Morgan up to date.

This suits Morgan and Hotoda just fine. They will now kidnap Maria and frame Hernandez for the deed. After extracting the Perfekto data from her sealed memory, they can kill her and Hernandez, planting the bodies with evidence that will convince investigators that Hernandez murdered his former star, and then committed suicide. A tragic loss to the music world.

This is the point where the player characters enter the story. First, they will have to deal with Sumiko Hotoda and her yakuza soldiers, who are assigned to kidnap Maria Mercurial. If they foil this threat, then Kyle Morgan and his cadre of "Dragon Knights" will attempt to save the mission. Morgan has a very big ace in the hole. His second-in-command is Perianwyr, an old friend with a taste for vintage rock and roll. Peri also happens to be a Western Dragon.

GETTING INTO IT

There are several good ways for getting the player characters into this adventure.

One way is for the gamemaster to have Max Foley contact one of the characters, offering a bodyguard job to that character and any other shadowrunners he thinks will be needed, at 5,000¥ apiece. If the character tries to dicker over the price, Foley asks him to wait until he knows the background and sets up a meet at Underworld 93, a hot rocker club, at 2:00 A.M. Foley will send them passes to get into the club.

Another possibility is that word is out on the streets that someone needs a team to handle some biz. Applicants are to contact a certain Fixer. If the team makes this contact, the Fixer provides passes to the club and instructs the player characters to go backstage at 2:00 A.M. for a meet with Max Foley.

Still another means is for a grateful former client or a friendly Contact to send the player characters passes for Maria's performance. Foley will notice the team (maybe he's heard about them through his street contacts), and he sends them an invitation to come backstage at 2:00 A.M.

Finally, the gamemaster can simply inform the characters that Maria Mercurial is appearing at Underworld 93. Let them know that she is one of the brightest stars in the rock heavens right now. Lacking passes, however, the group will just have to stand in line outside the club, along with all the other people trying to get in. Again, Foley will observe this likely group of hard-nosed shadowrunners, and get them into the club, inviting them to meet him backstage at 2:00 A.M.

Most of the characters will be delighted to discover that Maria Mercurial, one of the hottest rockers on the charts, is playing at the Underworld. Anyone with a taste for rock in the world of *Shadowrun* will be more than eager to catch a Mercurial club date.

Don't forget that all that's needed to get the adventure going is for the player characters to decide to check out Maria's show, one way or another. After that, the team will be off and running on their way into adventure!

UNDERWORLD 93

TELL IT TO THEM STRAIGHT

Anyone who knows the scene knows Underworld 93. The club started out as an industrial warehouse, and its cavernous interior is now a favorite spot for those who like their rock and roll meltdown-hot. Mixing with the novastars who rule the rock galaxy at the Underworld are newer bands, as owner Sidney Murdoch has a knack for identifying struggling young acts that later turn out to be chartbusters. Many of them show their gratitude by continuing to play the Underworld even when they could be filling one of Seattle's bigger halls for more money.

When you reach the club, the marquee over the main entrance spells out one word in meter-high Kromeglow letters: MERCURIAL. There's a mob outside, jostling for position at the door. A tough-looking Troll wearing a tuxedo is turning most of the hopefuls away, while private security guards patrol the area.

A smaller line to the left is for those with passes, which the guards are careful to scrutinize closely.

Flashes of multicolored light illuminate this scene from the windows of the battered warehouse building. People inside the club thoroughly enjoy watching the folks outside trying to get in. For some, it is a bigger rush than listening to the music.

BEHIND THE SCENES

If the player characters have passes, read the above description and then let them go straight in through the line at the left. If the characters are trying to get into the club via the main entrance, Newt, the Troll bouncer, will look them over and jerk his thumb, telling them to beat it. Almost at once, his pocket phone goes off, and after a brief conversation, he'll call the players' team back and let them in. Foley has contacted Newt and asked him to admit the team as his guests. Newt will glower forbiddingly at the characters and say "Awright, yer in. Enjoy da show and don't make no trouble. Dere's a guy wants ta talk at ya. Head backstage at 0200 and ask for Max. "

If anyone asks who is Max, Newt will shake his head in disbelief and tell the character that Max Foley is Maria Mercurial's manager. "Sheesh, doncha know nothin' about rock and roll, chummer?" He'll brush off any further questions on account of he's a little busy right now, O. K., chummer?

If the team is packing any firearms bigger than a pistol, they will have to check them at the door. If they refuse, it does not matter who invited them, they will not get in. If they kick up a fuss, half a dozen security guards will close in to quiet things down. If a major fight breaks out, the police patrols arrive in about five minutes. There are a lot of important people at the club tonight, and Lone Star does not want any incidents.

NEWT THE BOUNCER

Use the Troll Bouncer statistics from the **Shadowrun** basic rules, p. 173. Newt's nattily tailored evening clothes are woven of Armor Cloth, Ballistic 3, Impact 0 (Trolls also have 1 point of inherent Dermal Armor). Newt carries no firearms.

SECURITY GUARDS/LONE STAR COPS

Use the Street Cop statistics, **Shadowrun**, p. 171. All wear Armor Jackets, Ballistic 5, Impact 3. Given the high-density crowd situation, they will be reluctant to use deadly force.

There are twelve security guards on the scene. All are carrying Fichetti Security 500 pistols, loaded with Gel Rounds. These do 4L1 stun damage on a hit. Two guards are armed with Defiance Super Shock Tasers, and one guard is carrying a Defiance T-250 shotgun loaded with Stun Rounds doing 4M4 stun damage.

DEBUGGING

About the only thing that can go wrong is that the shadowrunners become stubborn about leaving their heavy weapons at the door. If that happens, they either get arrested and thrown in jail, or else end up on the run from the cops.

About the only way to debug such a mess is for Max Foley to contact the runners, either by paying their bail or through street Contacts if they are hiding out. He tells them they handled themselves well and sets up a meet at some neutral spot such as a bar or even a park. The action for the **Play It To The Max, Quicksilver Queen,** and **It's Shootout Time,** pp. 17-24, is set in this new scene.

If necessary, point out to the players that making trouble is not very intelligent under the circumstances. They can cool off before things get out of hand.

TELL IT TO THEM STRAIGHT

As you walk into the club, a middle-aged guy with a big gut, wearing a grungy Underworld 93 T-shirt, is standing center-stage, leading the applause for Low Earth Orbit, the warm-up band that's just finished its set. Anyone who follows the rock scene will recognize Sidney Murdoch, the club's owner. The place is jammed. Smoke fills the air so that the spotlight beams look like solid pillars of light. The bartenders are going berserk trying to keep up with the flow of orders.

"Right, you brain-damaged, re-wired mutants! Here's why you've been sweating all over my nice, clean floors all evening. Ladies and gentlemen—if there *are* any out there—and all the rest of you trash as well, here's MARIA MERCURIAL!"

The spotlights cut out, plunging the club into utter darkness as the crowd goes absolutely out of its mind. The applause goes on and on, until a single note starts to rise through the pitch darkness, getting louder and louder until it's almost at the threshold of pain. A searing white klieg light stabs down onto the stage, and reflects nova-bright off the silver skin of Maria Mercurial. She stands like a statue of molten white metal, as the rising note breaks suddenly into a driving, demanding rhythm, the intro to "Puta " the title song on her latest album. Suddenly, she is in motion, synthlinking the sound, driving it with her muscles and nerves. The club explodes into flashing lights, and the tri-vid wall behind the stage flashes with footage from the Toronto Food Riots of 2048. The music grabs you by the throat and screams at you:

> *Yo soy tu madre,* so don't frag with me,
> I'll mess you up bad if you dare disagree.
> My time is money, you know that, *cabrón.*
> You got what you wanted, so why hang around,
> *Yo soy tu madre.*
>
> Lovely *puta,* that's what you say to me,
> *Hola, puta,* I'm what you want me to be,
> Till you get the thing you want,
> Nothing's too good for me.
> But when you're done
> And have your fun, then it's
> *Puta,* dirty *puta,* just get away from me...

BEHIND THE SCENES

This section is intended mostly to set the scene. Maria's set runs for about an hour, with the audience members going wild at the end of it. After they finally calm down, Murdoch reminds them that Maria plays a second set at 2:00 A. M.

During the set, there is nothing much for the characters to do but kick back and enjoy the music. For one thing, no one wants to talk while Maria is singing, and for another, the volume is high enough to hammer any attempt at speech into the concrete dance floor.

After the set ends, the characters can continue to enjoy the club, as young bands on the rise share the reflected limelight of playing the same club date as Maria Mercurial.

If any of the shadowrunners try to find out more about Maria, Max Foley, or anything else, go to **Tellin Tales,** p. 16. If they just take it easy until 2:00 A. M. , proceed to **Play It To The Max,** p. 17.

UNDERWORLD 93 MAP KEY

Underworld 93 is a five-story tall, converted warehouse. The inside has been gutted out, and the cavernous interior still has a post-industrial, rust-belt look.

Areas 1–5 and 12–13 are built up to about three meters higher than street level. A sweeping ramp leads down to the main floor of the club.

CLUB ENTRANCE (1)

Two Kromeglow marquees tower up the walls, laying glowing letters over vids of the rockers who perform at the club. At the top of each marquee shines the Underworld 93 logo: Charon steering a high-powered speedboat across the River Styx.

MAIN DOORS (2)

Newt the Troll guards these, deciding who gets in and who gets turned away. Stairs lead up to the lobby.

PRIVATE ENTRANCE (3)

This entrance is for passholders, guests of the club, and other folks not subject to the hassle of rules and regs. Stairs lead up to the lobby.

COAT AND WEAPONS CHECK BOOTH (4)

An Armor Glass window connects the booth to the lobby.

THE LOBBY (5)

There is usually a press of people in here, meetin' and greetin'.

SPIRAL STAIRCASE (6)

This is one of several spiral staircases around the club that lead up to a bewildering array of catwalks, balconies, and booths attached to the walls or suspended over the main floor. Lining these areas are tables for those who prefer to not rub bodies down on the main floor. Windows let folks on the balconies look out at the folks trying to get in.

REST ROOMS (7)

THE BEAST! (8)

This is a complex, ten-meter high, bald, bullet-headed figure. Sidney Murdoch calls this the "mascot" of Underworld 93, but refuses to elaborate on this private joke. Lasers flash from the sculpture's eyes and its body is swathed in holograms, puffs of mist, and neolux tubing. A huge speaker in the statue's belly pounds out the music being played onstage. Subliminal images in the shimmering holos flash messages such as "Question Authority" or "Love is the Law" at onlookers. Unwary visitors to the Underworld have been known to become hypnotized by staring at the Beast too long.

TABLE AREA (9)

Crammed to capacity with tiny tables and chairs that must have been designed by the Spanish Inquisition, this area is usually crowded with people hovering to grab a table when one frees up.

THE BAR (10)

The bar is presided over by Tellin and staffed by a half-dozen barkeeps.

STOREROOM (11)

Stored here are items such as liquor, cleaning supplies, and glasses. The alcove outside the door, next to the bathrooms, is Tellin's "private office, " where he handles his little information exchanges.

SIDNEY MURDOCH'S OFFICE (12–13)

Area 12 is staffed by a receptionist. During the day, a couple of would-be rockers or their agents are usually sitting here waiting for an audition. Area 13 is Sidney's office. One wall is covered by a trid-screen, where Sidney can call up shots from various cameras scattered around the club.

DANCE FLOOR (14)

During Maria's sets, the floor is jammed, but most people are just jazzing in place while they listen to the music rather than really dancing. When the floor is in full flight, however, trying to cross it exposes you to a musical form of aggravated assault.

A broad ramp leads down to the dance floor from the upper level and lobby.

BACKSTAGE DOOR (15)

Desk and chair for the doorman.

THE STAGE (16)

Scattered about are a tangle of cables, music generators, synthlink interfaces, and so on. The stage is built about two meters higher than the dance floor. The front of the stage is roped off from the dance floor by railings, and the cleared area is jammed with speakers, laser generators, trid and vid units, mood blasters, and other hi-tech rocker toys. A bewildering array of lighting units hangs on trees and grids over the stage, as well as various grids hanging over the dance floor.

The enormous vidscreens (shown by the dotted lines) hang at the back of the stage, reaching almost to the ceiling of the cavernous club interior.

BACKSTAGE AREA (17)

See separate map in **It's Shootout Time**, p. 20.

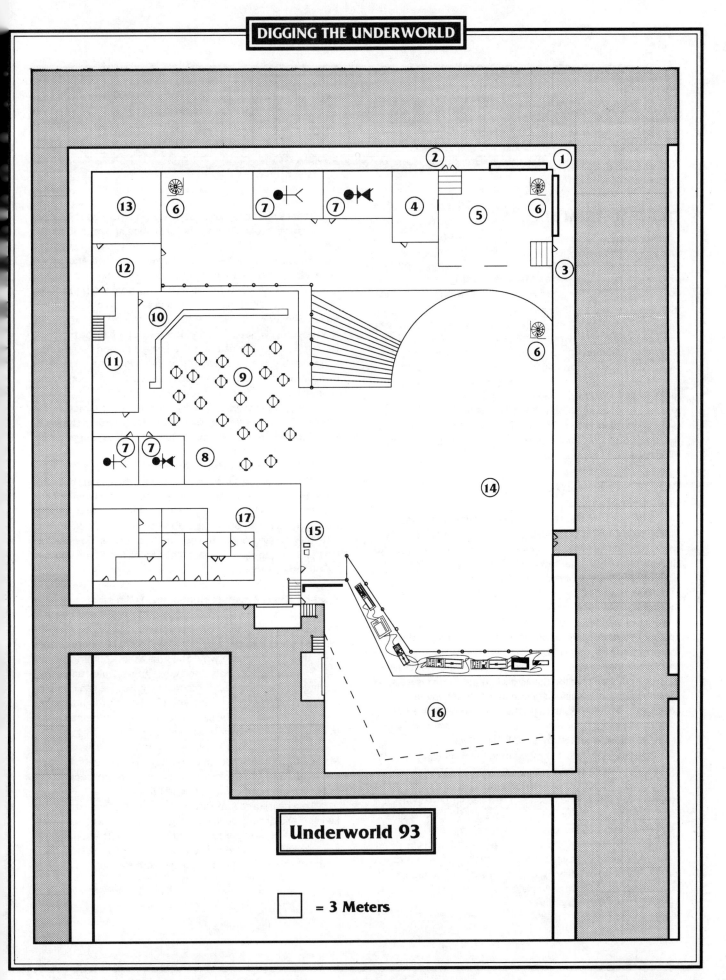

Underworld 93

☐ = 3 Meters

TELL IT TO THEM STRAIGHT

You wander about, striking up conversations. Every time you try to pump someone for information or simply get the discussion past "Golly-gee, Maria is wizard, ain't she," the conversation dies. The speaker won't know more about Maria than you can read off the news-nets.

One or two will react to Max Foley's name. They tell you he's a big-name agent who recently signed Maria Mercurial after she broke with her long-time manager, Armando Hernandez. Most of them will show distaste when speaking of Foley.

Finally, someone mentions that the guy who knows all the dirt is Tellin, the club's chief bartender. They point out a tall, typically handsome Elf behind the central bar.

As you walk over to him, he looks up with a sly smile and gestures you to join him in an alcove next to the bar. "I've been expecting you," he murmurs.

BEHIND THE SCENES

Tellin is aware that Foley has been looking for muscle, and that he has, one way or another, set up the meet with the player characters. Because he also knows that everyone who comes to Underworld 93 for information will eventually come to him, he has, indeed, been expecting this discussion.

Tellin is kind of like a vending machine. Put the money in the slot if you want to get what he has to offer. Fifty nuyen lets a player character ask a question. If Tellin does not have an answer, the player gets to ask again. The only information that matters to the adventure concerns three people: Maria Mercurial, Max Foley, and Armando Hernandez. If the gamemaster desires, Tellin can give the characters information in response to questions on other subjects that may not be of any use in the adventure. Remember, though, that it comes at 50¥ a pop.

If asked about Maria Mercurial, Tellin says:

"She played her first set right here in this club, in '47. Her agent then was Armando Hernandez, and he camped in Murdoch's waiting room for a week, trying to get him to set up an audition. But wow, when Sidney heard her sing, that was all it took. He booked her on an open contract, for as long as she wanted to stay. Six weeks later, she got her first recording contract and the rest, like they say, is history. But she never forgets her friends, like you can see tonight. She could pull down a drekload of nuyen playing the Dome or some other big hall, but she comes to Seattle and plays a place like the Underworld instead. That's class, chummer.

"What's she really like? Depends on what day it is, man. Well, you've probably read the drek they shovel out on the rocker channels. She's got problems, more than most. One minute, she's the rocker queen to the max, hard and super-hype, on hyperdrive to the nova, O. K. ? The next, she's locked up inside herself like some uptight biddy from the burbs. Like, she even talks different, get me? She's not a total brainwipe. I mean, she doesn't forget what she said or did when she changes. But I've seen it before. There's a lot of it in the business. That lady must have had herself a heavy habit on dreamchips. I think she's gotta be clean, or that drek would have killed her by now. But she was jacking some bad stuff once upon a time, chummer. Take it from someone who knows."

The gamemaster may wish to give the characters the _Rocker Stars_ interview at this point, for it shows the well-loved Maria in the grip of one of her least charming persona.

If asked about Max Foley, Tellin says:

"The man knows the business, better than most, but what a jerk! He's found some hot bands, and helped them make it big, but after a few years, they usually split and find another manager, 'cause he pulls some drek that ticks them off no end.

"Still, Foley is one of the best in the business, no question. If he's looking to sign you on, hit him for all the nuyen you can. He oughtta be rolling in it."

If asked about Armando Hernandez, Tellin says:

"A pretty good track record as a manager, and he's had some hot bands, but once Maria's career took off, he gave the rest of his acts to other agents and worked with her exclusive. Well, drek, you can see why. She's novastar, chummer.

"Hernandez is a pretty good guy, I guess. Quiet, unless he's putting on the act getting a contract signed. He can come on pretty strong. He's Hispanic, y'know? I think he mighta moved here from Aztlan a while back, and he still does the _machismo_ thing if someone tries to push him around.

"I gotta say, I don't know what he did to hose his deal with Maria. Maybe he just couldn't do enough for her career. Her new manager, Foley, is a sleaze-bag, but he has the right connections to hype a top act the way it oughtta be.

"I did hear some rumbling on the street that Hernandez was taking it pretty hard. Maria leaving to work with Foley, I mean. Maybe that he was gonna try and do something about it...run some shadows in on them, y'know? Nuyen to nutrisoy, that's what Foley wants to talk to you chummers about."

TELL IT TO THEM STRAIGHT

Finally, it's 0200, showtime for you as well as Maria. As she comes onstage for her second set and the audience goes into wild applause, you are able to slip through the crowd unobserved, heading toward the stage door.

A burly dwarf is seated at a small table beside the stage door. It has a big sign in glowing red letters that almost shouts, "Authorized Personnel Only. And That Means YOU!"

The dwarfish doorman wears a royal blue, satin-textured jacket, padded at the shoulders, covered with holoprint dragons that chase each other around the fabric. The design is almost gaudy enough to hide the bulge under his left arm. He glances at you over mirrored shades. "You must be the guys to see Foley. Dressing Room Number One, left and down to the end of the hall. Last door on the right. " He waves you through the door.

Backstage, the music still reverberates loudly. You can see a couple of stagehands sitting around, waiting for the set to end so they can break down the equipment for the night. Most of the other folks, band members, roadies, and such, are out front, digging Maria's act.

Left and down the hall, you pass half-a-dozen numbered doorways before you come to Number One. If you knock, a voice from within yells, "It's open. " Pushing the door open, you find yourself in a dressing room.

Seated in a chair in the corner is a short, tubby man, about 50, wearing clothes designed for someone at least 30 years younger. He's got rings on most of his fingers and is wearing a mass of gold jewelry that looks like it might be real. He is smoking a fat, greenish cigar.

"C'mon in, " he says. "Gladdameetcha, I'm Max Foley. You're on time. Good. That's the mark of a pro. I mean, punctuality, am I right? Hey, can I get you guys anything?"

After giving out drinks, wheezes, smoggers, and other such homely entertainments, Foley tells his story to the team.

"Now Maria looks tough, but take it from me, inside that metal skin is one vulnerable little girl. She just don't know how business is done sometimes. We're all sophisticated people here, am I right? Well, to slot this and run it, Maria used to be represented by Armando Hernandez. Hernandez and me, well, we both go back a long way in this biz, and I gotta tell ya, we don't usually see eye to eye. You know how that is. Some folks, they can see business is business, others gotta make everything personal, am I right? I dunno why that is. Hernandez came up here from Aztlan, and Azzies, they got this macho thing, am I right? They just can't let nobody win over them. Even though Hernandez is a UCAS cit now, he still carries this Azzie macho thing around.

"Last month, Maria she comes to me and tells me she's had it with this Hernandez guy, O. K. ? She found he was in pretty tight with the yak, and some pretty dirty biz at that. Dreamchips, you know? BTLs the kids call them —"Better Than Life. " That's what those poor drekheads think. That stuff burns your brain to Gel-Slurp, am I right? So she wants to dump Hernandez as her manager. Who wouldn't? She knows I'm the only agent with the connections to give a talent like her the right exposure.

"So that's wizard. I ain't gonna kick if a mega-novastar wants to come work with me. We sign the contracts, she gives Hernandez a statutory 30 days notice of her intent, and that oughtta be all there is to it.

"But that Hernandez, he's gotta make it personal. He sends around a punker to give Maria a message…no, not a message, a fragging ultimatum. She works for him, he says, or she don't work at all, she never works again, the creep says! Maria busts up the punker, but we're both worried. Hernandez made it pretty clear he wasn't just talking lawsuits here. Drek, he ain't gotta leg to stand on legally, but he's connected, am I right? I mean, the guy's talking muscle.

"Now, legally, Maria still works under Hernandez's agency for five more days. For those five days, I can't really bring any leverage to bear on Hernandez to back off. After that, the guild comes in on my side, and Hernandez so much as looks crosseyed at me or Maria, he's history in this business. But we need protection for five days. That's why I wanted to talk to you guys. This is what you do, isn't it? I can go five grand for each of you. That's a grand a day. Not bad money, am I right?"

BEHIND THE SCENES

This is a good time to let the team ask questions, go back and fill in blanks, and so on. Foley will stick to the story as he has told it. He does not know anything more about Hernandez's apparent yakuza connection. That is Maria's concern, and they'll have to ask her about it.

At this point, he is also willing to talk price. He will not try to cut the price from 5,000¥ per character, but if they want it higher, it is negotiation time. Max will react as though they want him to cut out his heart if they press for more money.

"Ah c'mon guys, you're killing me with this stuff. I'm just a businessman like you, trying to protect an investment. Hey, you probably think rockers, they're rich, they're rolling in nuyen, am I right? Honest chummers, you're gonna break the bank!" And so on. Roleplay this if you can. Jump up and down, scream, throw things. Ideally, the shadowrunners will respond the same way. ("Hey chummer, you want muscle. You don't get squat paying these street-corner prices, y'dig?")

The players should choose the character they want to handle the bargaining, presumably the one with the best Negotiation Skill. He makes an Opposed Success Test using his Negotiation Skill against Foley's Negotiation Skill of 7 (see **Shadowrun,** p. 59).

If the players pleased the gamemaster with their roleplaying during the bargaining, the gamemaster might reduce their Target Number by 1 or 2 points.

If the players succeed in the test, every net success increases the offer by 500¥ per team member. Foley will react to any increase in the price as if he is being forced to cut off an arm or leg to satisfy the team. If the players fail the test, Foley will stand firm on his offer.

If the team instead makes a pitch for extra money to cover *expenses* (including medical costs), then for every success rolled, Maxie will cover 1,000¥ per member in legitimate expenses, such as special gear, ammo, and medical treatment.

After the negotiation, Foley will make another pitch *if the players' team includes a decker!* This subplot does not help the characters unless they have a decker on board.

"Wow, you guys are tough in a bargain. Tell ya what I'm gonna do. Hernandez is slime, am I right? Now me, I try to keep professional courtesy, but Hernandez, what does he know from courtesy? I wasn't sure I wanted to raise this little issue, but Hernandez is holding out 180 grand in fees from Maria's concerts last month. He just won't pay her the money, and you folks saw how that little lady earns her pay. I mean, she has it coming, am I right?

"Now I happen to know Hernandez isn't keeping this credit in his own account. I mean, would a sleaze like that keep the money where my own accountants could find it? No way, am I right? No, he's got Maria's fees stashed in a tin-plated, rinky-dink operation called Federated Funds Net over on Twelfth Avenue. A lot of folks in the business use it, because their tax-reporting and record-keeping is, well…let's just say they understand some of the demands that show business can make on cash flow, O. K. ?

"Now, I happen to know Federated's system address and Hernandez's account code. I don't normally hold with datasteals, you understand, but this time, well, if the other fella doesn't play by the rules, what can you do, am I right? If the funds that Maria's got coming to her were to be redirected to my bank account, well, I could see my way to a finder's fee of, say, 10 percent?"

If the decker is interested, Foley will give him Federated's system address on LTG #7206, Hernandez's account code, and a one-way, deposit-only access code to feed the credit to his bank, via his own computer, which is on LTG #9206. The decker can perform this operation in the Federated Funds net CPU or in the Datastore that holds Hernandez's account file.

Foley doesn't have to "launder" the deposit, as Maria can initiate court proceedings to retain it after her contract with Hernandez legally expires.

If the team is interested in Foley's offer, they can shake hands with their new Mr. Johnson.

DEBUGGING

The obvious problem that can arise here is that the shadowrunners refuse Foley's offer. If negotiations are breaking down, inform the players that the music has finished playing and that thunderous applause is coming from the club. Maria has finished her set. Before they can leave, the door of the dressing room flies open, and in walks Maria Mercurial. Proceed to the next section, **Quicksilver Queen,** p. 19. If meeting Maria does not capture the runners' interest enough to make them take the job and they start to leave, proceed immediately to the action in **It's Shootout Time,** p. 20. The firefight and its aftermath will leave the shadowrunners in company with Max and Maria, all on the run together.

QUICKSILVER QUEEN

TELL IT TO THEM STRAIGHT

As you close the deal with Foley, you notice that the music, which has been audible in the background until now, has stopped playing, and that sounds of thunderous applause are echoing backstage from the club. Sounds like Maria has finished playing her set.

Every red-blooded, male metahuman in the room is going to have to take a deep breath. The rocker princess is even more charismatic at close quarters than she is on stage. She is still high on the adrenalin surge of a star performer, and prowls the tiny room like a lithe, silver panther. She radiates sexuality and a strong tang of danger. She is abrupt, energized, as though preparing for battle.

GAMEMASTER'S NOTE: At this point, Maria's Amazon personality, her usual persona during a performance, is in charge.

Her English is excellent, with a noticeable Aztlan accent. If she becomes excited, Maria begins to mix Aztec and Spanish with her English.

After being introduced to the team, she steps into the bathroom to clean up and change. When she emerges, she is subdued, speaking quietly and factually, with little emotion. The tight, revealing costume she wore on stage has been replaced by a padded kimono, belted tightly around the waist. Though she is as attractive as ever, there is none of the flaunting, sexual challenge that she gave off before.

GAMEMASTER'S NOTE: Maria's Schoolmistress personality is now in effect, and will remain so until the fighting begins in the next section.

If the shadowrunners ask Maria about the situation, she will tell them:

"I was very happy working with Armando. He took a frightened and angry child, singing for pennies in a brothel, and showed her how to give fear and anger a voice to cry out. He helped me to make a career, and…in other ways was a good friend.

"Most of all, he did not look at me like a freak with a metal body, or as a thing to take to his bed, but as another human being, lost in this world we must all live in. We were never lovers, but if he had ever asked or wanted to, I think…

"Well, that is past now. Five years we worked together. Last month, our office computer had a crash. While working to restore the data, I found files from Armando's private memory space. They implicated him in the dreamchip traffic. I lost…someone close to me to the…the dreams. I could not bear to be so near someone who sold that death to people. It was worse,

perhaps, because Armando was someone I loved, someone I respected. Yes, I owed him much, but this, no, it could not be tolerated. So I came to *Señor* Foley. The relationship is just—" with a sidelong glance of distaste at Max "—just business. But that is perhaps better, no? The heart is not involved off the stage, and so can sing all the more clearly for that. "

Maria can add little more to this picture of why she left Hernandez, and she will absolutely refuse to speak of her life before she met him and began her climb to the top of the rocker heap. She cannot produce the incriminating documents, because she erased them before walking out of Hernandez's office forever. She will refuse to answer questions about her cyberwork.

BEHIND THE SCENES

Before running this section, review the description of Maria in **Cast of Characters**. She will tend to slip from personality to personality in dealing with questions, especially stressful ones. **The Cast of Characters** section includes suggestions for role-playing this complex character.

An important point in any question-and-answer with Maria is that she will not admit that she has used dreamchips, nor that she has lost all memory of her life before the therapy that helped her kick the habit. The trauma surrounding these facts is intensely painful to both her psyche and her pride, and her psychological defenses against that pain are very strong.

Confused and hurt by Hernandez's apparent trafficking in the thing she hates most, Maria is not entirely rational on the subject, and the shadowrunners will not have much time to try to get her to examine these events logically before events jump into overdrive in the next section.

DEBUGGING

Again, the worst that can happen is that the shadowrunners decide not to take the mission. One way the gamemaster might try to change their minds is to let Maria switch into her Innocent personality, rather sad and wistful, when she asks for their help. If this appeal to sentiment does not work, and they start to leave, proceed directly to the next section. Gunplay may talk louder than vulnerability.

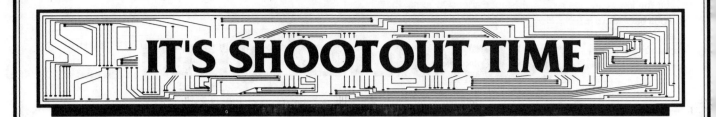

IT'S SHOOTOUT TIME

TELL IT TO THEM STRAIGHT

Suddenly the door of the dressing room crashes open. There are two guys in the doorway, dressed identically: long vinyl slickers that are probably Lined Coats, heavy engineer boots, bone-white skin dye, bleached hair greased into the Bed O' Nails look that's hot this week. Both are armed and shooting.

All of you see one thing, for sure! Their eyes are glowing a deep, bloody red. Well, you may think, that's no big deal. I can make my cybereyes glow red too, right? Yeah, chummers, but these guys ain't GOT cybereyes.

The first guy in through the shattered door yells something in Spanish (actually, in a gutter dialect).

GAMEMASTER'S NOTE: If one of the player characters speaks Spanish, he should make an Unresisted Success Test for that skill, with a Target Number 3. If the roll is successful, the character knows that the guy said, "You were warned, chica. Don't frag with Hernandez!"

It's shootout time!

BEHIND THE SCENES

There are three attackers, street samurai hired by Sumiko Hotoda, the yakuza hitmage. She has instructed them to kidnap Maria and to kill anyone else with her. They have been ordered *not* to kill Maria! Sumiko does not actually expect them to succeed. She knows Foley is "interviewing" shadowrunners tonight, and this attack is meant to implicate Hernandez in front of witnesses. If the attack succeeds, fine, they will have Maria and the plan can proceed. If her street killers die in the attempt, null perspiration, chummer. They have still achieved their objective, for now the surviving shadowrunners will think that Hernandez ordered a deadly attack on his former protégée.

But what happens if the street samurai get captured and interrogated, or maybe try to escape if they start losing? Well, Sumiko wondered about that, too, so she has drugged the samurai with Pugnacine-Beta. This makes them incapable of pain or fear in battle. She also has them under a spell that lets her keep tabs on their actions. That is what makes their eyes glow. Of course, the Pugnacine will probably kill them when it wears off.

Samurai #1 and #2 come through the door while #3 covers the hall outside. They have already subdued any NPCs (roadies, stage hands, et al.) who were backstage (two dead, three severely injured).

The gamemaster may, of course, have the attackers use any tactics, or may use the following possible attack plan. In the initial attack, Samurai #1 kneels in the doorway, sweeping the room with fire from his Uzi III. Samurai #2 stands behind him,

firing the Roomsweeper over his head. Samurai #3 will advance to the doorway only if one of the first two goes down in the first two turns. Otherwise, he stands in the hallway, in front of the doorway to a dressing room (12). He will fire at anyone who exits Maria's dressing room, except Maria herself.

SAMURAI ATTACK

Each player should make an Unresisted Success Test using his Reaction Rating. The Target Number is 4.

0 Successes	The character is totally surprised. All he can do for the first turn of combat is attempt to dodge their shots. The character does not even have a chance to pull out his weapons until next turn.
1 Success	The character can dodge, move, and so on normally, but all his tests for the first turn are at +2 to their Target Numbers because of the suddenness of the action.
2 Successes	The character can react normally.
3+ Successes	The character can see that the first guy through the doorway is carrying an Uzi III. The guy behind him carries a Remington Roomsweeper. In addition, the character can see at least one more goon dressed the same as these two. This third attacker is moving out of the line of sight of the doorway, presumably to cover the hallway.

Eyes of the Pack Spell (Detection)
Drain: S1   **Type:** Mana   **Duration:** Sustained
Special Effects:

This spell requires voluntary subjects. It is an Area Spell, affecting all voluntary subjects in range. The subjects become "cameras." As long as the magician maintains the spell, he can see through the eyes of any member of "the pack." The spell causes the subjects' eyes to glow, as though reflecting the flash of a camera, all the time. Maximum "reception" range is the caster's Magic x Spell Force x 10 meters.

If the killers are still facing resistance after two turns, they will pull back into the hall. Samurai #2 and Samurai #3 cover the door, while Samurai #1 tosses a concussion grenade into the dressing room. They plan to potshot their targets as they try to escape from the room. It is true that this plan might endanger Maria, but any goons filled up with berserker drugs are bound to be a little fuzzy on orders not to harm certain people.

If the grenade trick fails, the samurai will try to take the shadowrunners out in a frontal assault. Combat should continue until all the samurai are down. If knocked out, they will remain unconscious until the Pugnacine wears off an hour or so later, whereupon they will die of severe systemic shock.

While playing the samurai, there are several things to keep in mind. First, the samurai will not show any signs of pain or shock when wounded. The drug does not prevent wounds from affecting them, but it suppresses any pain reflexes.

Second, the drug makes them fight to the death. They also do things like shoot on full auto into a melee, even if it means hitting one of their own guys.

Third, if a samurai is examined astrally, it becomes evident that he is under a spell. If the magician wishes to assense the spell, he or she makes an Unresisted Sorcery Skill Test with a Target Number 4.

ASSENSING THE SAMURAI

1–2 Successes	The spell is identified as a Detection Spell.
3 Successes	The character learns the spell is at Force 5.
4-5 Successes	This is a "non-published" spell that lets the caster see things through the eyes of the subject.
6+ Successes	If the magician is this lucky, the gamemaster might also flash him a picture of a beautiful Japanese woman in a severely tailored business suit, weaving her hands in magical gestures. This means the magician has picked up an image from the samurai's memory of Sumiko casting the spell.

Of course, whether the shadowrunners notice the spell or not, Sumiko sees anything her goons see. Therefore, she probably sees the characters and would be able to describe them to others and recognize them again in the future.

The samurai fight until they are all down. As soon as the fighting ends, begin the action in the next section, **The Stars Are Shining**.

If a shaman wants to summon a spirit to help fight the samurai, he will get Underworld 93's Hearth Spirit, which is described below.

Pugnacine-Beta

This drug was originally developed as part of a Soviet program in the early part of the 21st century. The researchers were after a compound that would increase the efficiency of soldiers in combat. Pugnacine-Beta has the following effects and side-effects:

- Subjects are rendered paranoid and tend to go berserk in combat.
- Subjects do not suffer effects of fatigue until it incapacitates them. That is, Mental Damage imposes no penalties until all ten boxes on the Mental Condition Monitor are filled.
- Subjects do not feel physical pain. The effects of Physical Damage are normal, but subjects do not show any sign of pain from wounds.
- Subjects suffer massive system-shock when the drug wears off, with a 95 percent chance of fatal coronary, cerebral hemorrhage, or similar incident.
- Subjects have their Willpower reduced to 1.

The collapse of the Soviet bloc put an end to the research. The drug is not widely used in the Awakened world because its effect on Willpower makes subjects so vulnerable to magic. It is used mostly by criminal and intelligence communities for various covert operations. Strike teams treated with Pugnacine-Beta are, of course, considered expendable. The drug's high lethality does tend to ensure that captured users will not be around long enough to crack under interrogation. Some organizations regard this as an advantage.

UNDERWORLD 93 HEARTH SPIRIT

This hearth spirit would be summoned by any shaman using his Conjuring Skill inside Underworld 93 (**Shadowrun**, p. 85). It manifests at whatever Force the shaman uses to summon it. This will be its rating for all Attributes. The spirit appears as a small humanoid, about a meter tall. It is wearing black denim jeans, pointy-toed boots set with silver skulls, and a bulky leather jacket covered with zippers and chains. It also wears mirrored sunglasses, a heavy ring in its left ear, and has its hair in dreadlocks. The spirit carries a solid-gold electric guitar, with the word "FENDER" spelled out in diamonds.

Besides the usual powers of its kind, the Hearth Spirit can play ear-splittingly loud chords on its guitar. This attack always hits its target, and requires the target to make a Willpower Resistance Test against (Force)M2 stun damage. It can affect any and all people in the area with this attack.

If treated with great courtesy, the spirit may take a liking to the shaman who conjures it (especially if the guy is knowledgeable about rock and roll and at least marginally cool). In such case, the spirit may invite the shaman to drop by for a chat, but only "after you've got your act together, dude. This shootin' and killin' stuff just ain't my bag, know what I mean? Peace, love, and waterbeds!" Spirits often speak ancient tongues, and this one talks in late-20th century rocker slang. The gamemaster may also find this an intriguing hook for future adventures.

DEBUGGING

One obvious problem can occur here. If the samurai kill off all the player characters, the adventure ends before it even gets rolling. So, if the fight seems to be going against the shadowrunners, and they are losing badly, the gamemaster can:

- Let Maria's Amazon persona take over. She will pull out her Browning Max-Power and start to fire away.
- Have Newt and Tellin show up, armed to the teeth. Newt attacks Samurai #3 from behind, using a large axe(treat as pole arm), while Tellin is sniping away with an assault rifle from a trapdoor in the ceiling.

In either case, it is not necessary to roll dice for the NPCs' part of the fight, for this is "sending in the cavalry, " pure and simple. If things reach this stage, the player characters definitely need rescuing. Have the "good guys" win, that is, Maria and/or Tellin and Newt wipe out the goons.

If a shadowrunner is down and dying, and none of the other runners has Biotech Skill, Tellin shows up in the next section, **The Stars Are Shining,** if he's not already present. There will not be time for any lengthy doctoring, but he can certainly patch up the characters. Someone has reported the gunfire to the cops, and as Newt tells them in the next section, the stars are shining brightly in Underworld 93.

BACKSTAGE AT UNDERWORLD 93 MAP KEY

The backstage area is a flimsy construction inside the cavernous interior of Underworld 93. It is about four meters high, built entirely of Normal Construction Plastic (Barrier Rating 4).

ENTRANCE (1)
Guarded by a doorman.

LOUNGE AREA 2)
Battered sofas and chairs, with a rank of vending machines to one side.

STAGE MIRROR (3)
A three-paneled, full-length mirror, with FlexiLux™ spotlights mounted on top. A control console lets the user set the spotlight color and intensity to check costume and makeup before going on.

A simple synthlink interface allows the user to jack in and check effects using the kind of pulsing, changing lights he or she will use on stage.

MASTER CONTROL AND PATCH CONSOLE (4)
This complex system controls the master settings for all lights, music systems, and other effect-generators in the club, and slaves them to performer control, as needed.

STORAGE AREA (5)
Stored here are packing materials for touring acts, plus racks of spare lights, speakers, amps, and other equipment. In the cabinet marked with a red cross is a Medikit.

STORAGE AREA (6–7)
More storage, mostly for equipment such as tools and electronic and microtronic gear.

DRESSING ROOMS (8–12)
These dressing rooms are small and cramped, with one or two dressing tables and a closet in each. Rooms 8–10 share a single bathroom, as do rooms 11–12.

MARIA'S DRESSING ROOM (13)
Dressing Room Number One, reserved for the current star act. Larger and more comfortable than the others, the room has a private bath, stage mirror, small bar, trideo system, practice synthlink interface and music generator, and so on. This is where the shadowrunners will meet Max and Maria, and where the fight with the Street Samurai will begin.

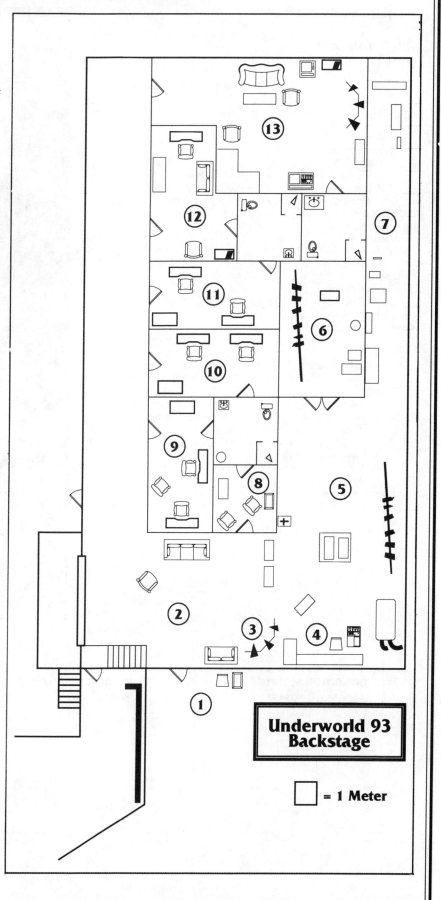

Underworld 93
Backstage

☐ = 1 Meter

OTHER NPCS

STREET SAMURAI

Attributes

Body: 4(5)*
Quickness: 4
Strength: 4
Charisma: 2
Intelligence: 2
Willpower: 1**
Essence: 3.3
Reaction: 3 (5)***

*Body is increased by +1 due to Dermal Plating.
**Willpower reduced to 1 by injection of Pugnacine-Beta
***Wired Reflexes increase Reaction by +2, and the samurai roll 2D6 for initiative.

Skills:

Firearms: 6
Unarmed Combat: 6

Dice Pools:

Dodge: 4
Defense (Armed): 1
Defense (Unarmed): 6

Cyberware:

Dermal Plating: 1
Retractable Razors (Damage 2L2)
Wired Reflexes: 1

Gear:

All three are wearing chic, black vinylite Lined Coats: Ballistic 4, Impact 2.

Samurai #1: Uzi III SMG. Ammo 16 (Clip). Damage 4M3. Equipped with Laser Sight (–1 to Target Number to hit). 1 extra clip.

Samurai #2: Remington Roomsweeper Shotgun (Heavy Pistol). Ammo 6 (Magazine). Damage 2M4. Loading flechette shells (already factored into damage figure). This means Ballistic Armor Effects are *halved*, but that Impact Armor Effects are *doubled*. Targets gain the benefit of whichever armor has the higher value. Samurai #2 carries a dozen loose rounds in his pocket.

Samurai #3: AK97 Assault Carbine. Ammo 22 (Clip). Damage 5M3. Laser Sight gives him –1 to Target Number to hit. He carries 1 extra clip. Samurai #3 also carries a Super Shock Taser (**Shadowrun,** p. 120) for use in subduing Maria for capture.

All three also carry Ares Predators. Ammo 10 (Clip). Damage 4M4. Loading Explosive Ammo (already factored into damage figure).

Each also carries one Concussion Grenade.

CONDITION MONITOR

	MENTAL	PHYSICAL	
Unconscious.> Possibly dead	☐	☐	< Unconscious. Further damage causes wounds.
Seriously > Wounded.	☐	☐	< Seriously Fatigued.
Moderately > Wounded.	☐	☐	< Moderately Fatigued.
Lightly > Wounded.	☐	☐	< Lightly Fatigued.

CONDITION MONITOR

	MENTAL	PHYSICAL	
Unconscious.> Possibly dead	☐	☐	< Unconscious. Further damage causes wounds.
Seriously > Wounded.	☐	☐	< Seriously Fatigued.
Moderately > Wounded.	☐	☐	< Moderately Fatigued.
Lightly > Wounded.	☐	☐	< Lightly Fatigued.

CONDITION MONITOR

	MENTAL	PHYSICAL	
Unconscious.> Possibly dead	☐	☐	< Unconscious. Further damage causes wounds.
Seriously > Wounded.	☐	☐	< Seriously Fatigued.
Moderately > Wounded.	☐	☐	< Moderately Fatigued.
Lightly > Wounded.	☐	☐	< Lightly Fatigued.

THE STARS ARE SHINING

TELL IT TO THEM STRAIGHT

Newt and Tellin come running up the corridor. Newt looks around and grunts, "Whadda pile of oozin' drek! Youse chummers best buzz turbo, 'cause da stars is shinin' all over da place an' da Underwoild don't need no heat! Out front's too bright for shadows, but backside's clean fer now. C'mon! Whaddya waitin' for? Slot it and run it, O. K. !" He seems quite upset.

GAMEMASTER'S NOTE: If the players do not move at once, Tellin will give a sigh and say:

"Let me translate. He said: 'Oh my, what an unfortunate occurrence! You fellows had better depart quickly, because the agents of Lone Star Security are present in force, and Underworld 93 prefers to avoid any official scrutiny! The front of the club is too heavily patrolled for a covert exit, but the back entrance is presently unobserved. Come now! Why do you delay? Make haste, if you would be so kind. '"

The two make it clear that the cops will arrive any second, and anyone still on the scene is going to have to answer some pointed questions: "Do you always carry automatic weapons when you go to a bar?" "Just what is your SIN, citizen?"

Meanwhile, you notice that Maria is curled up, almost in fetal position, sobbing softly. Foley is staring, glassy-eyed, at the whole mess. He turns to you and says, "Some kind of macho thing, am I right?" He faints dead away.

BEHIND THE SCENES

The point of this whole sequence is to get the shadowrunners out of the club, in company with Max and Maria.

As for Newt and Tellin, in addition to informing the player characters that the cops are about to arrive, they serve several other functions:

- Newt has brought along any gear the shadowrunners checked when they entered the club.
- Tellin has a Biotech Skill of 7. In a potentially rough place like a club, the bartender has to keep the customers alive or else business suffers, right? He will dig out the first aid kit from the Storage Area and patch up anyone in bad shape.
- If the runners walked to the club or if they cannot carry Max and Maria on their vehicles, or if, for some reason, they do not have a vehicle, Newt will cuss and then pull out the keys to his van. Grabbing a runner by the lapels, he shoves the keys into his hand, and snarls, "Lime-green van wit' da poiple racin' stripe, parked in da alley. Dis ain't on accounta youse. It's on accounta her. " This last with a nod toward Maria, who is still very out of it. "Get her outta dis, chummer, and fast. An' if youse so much as scratch da paint, I'll, I'll…aaaah gedoutta heah!"

Unless the players are very stubborn or very foolish ("Hey, it's our civic duty to report this to the authorities!"), the characters should get away.

The gamemaster should keep two things in mind about Max's actions once he revives:

- Under no circumstances will he agree to turn this matter over to the police. "Hey, what am I paying you guys for? What can the cops do? You saw what happened, am I right? That fraggin' Hernandez, he sends these yak-mumbo-zombo-spook-killers after us. Hey, this is the mob we're fighting! Cops can't protect you from the yak, am I right? Ya gotta fight fire with fire. "
- He will be open to further negotiations to increase the price. He is so frightened now that the thought of spending the extra money is not so distasteful to him. Use the Negotiation rules in **Play It To The Max**, p. 17, but the Target Number is only 5. Max will not, of course, volunteer to increase the price. He may be scared, but he's not crazy! The shadowrunners will have to raise the issue.

Once out of the club, whether on their own or in the hands of the police, the team must decide what to do next. In the next section, **On the Run**, they soon learn that life out on the streets is getting too hot to handle.

DEBUGGING

Two possible problems could crop up: Either the shadowrunners get picked up by Lone Star, or they decide not to take the job.

If the characters get hauled in for questioning, then Maria, Max, Tellin, Newt, and everyone else with them gets busted, too. They all end up sitting in the local precinct's holding cell for a couple of hours. Statements are taken. Entries are made in computer records. Those without SINs may have serious discussions with the officers in the back room of the station house (requiring a Body Resistance Test against 4M3 stun damage). Cops don't like shadows.

If any of the characters have contacts with the police, this is a good time to make use of someone like a friendly lieutenant.

Alternatively, after statements are taken and everyone is arraigned, the district attorney can decide not to prosecute such an obvious case of self-defense.

Finally, the gamemaster can have Max cough up bail for himself, Maria, and the characters. Bail is 500¥ each, and would count as "expenses" if Foley's deal with the team covered them.

If the characters decide not to take the job, there is not much more the gamemaster can do but put the story on hold and try to find out why the players are unenthusiastic about the adventure.

If the shadowrunners have already accepted the contract, then point out to them that backing out of a contract will ruin their reputation on the street. Who will ever hire them again for *anything* if they let a firefight with some punkers scare them off? For that matter, if they still have not decided to take the job, point out that if they back out now, it will look like Hernandez's goons scared them off.

If neither Max's money, Maria's distress, nor concern for their own reputations can persuade them to take the run, something is very wrong here. Until the gamemaster gets some honest feedback from the players, he's likely to be at an impasse. Once he finds out their objections, he can try to resolve them. If that is not possible, go to **Picking Up The Pieces** and read clipping #1 to them. End of story.

ON THE RUN

TELL IT TO THEM STRAIGHT

You've got some decisions to make, shadowrunners. You've got an hysterical booking agent and a nearly catatonic rock star on your hands. What's more, you've ticked off the cops and there may be yakuza soldiers out on the streets looking for you.

Max has a few ideas: "Holy crud, you guys, what are you waiting for? Go out and find that fragger Hernandez and shoot his butt! Whaddaya gonna sit around, waiting for him to send in more goons, or what! The best defense is a good offense, am I right?"

Maria is very withdrawn. She grabbed a small case from the dressing room before she collapsed, and has been holding onto it tightly ever since. If left to herself, she will eventually open it and jack into the small synthlink and keyboard unit the case contains. She clips on a set of headphones and sits hunched over the keyboard, making music. If anyone asks to listen, she silently hands him a second pair of earphones. The sound could tear your heart out.

She has no suggestions about what to do next. The emotional pressures of the past few hours have drained her. Synthlinking is how she rebuilds her strength.

A phone rings. Maybe it is someone's pocket unit, maybe a built-in job. On the line is an old Contact, someone who owes you one. "Geez, you guys are hot. The word is out on the street. Someone is willing to pop 10,000¥ for info on you and the people you're with. Better go to ground, chummer, 'cause you're big time biz right now." The Contact hangs up before you can ask for any other details.

All right, chummers, what do you do now?

BEHIND THE SCENES

This section represents a crossroads in the adventure. At this juncture, events can go in several different directions as the characters try to stay alive while on the run. Each of the next four sections describes how the shadowrunners can obtain information about what is going on. One way or another, though, anything they do from now on will eventually lead to the showdown with Sumiko Hotoda and her yakuza soldiers in **Yakkity Yak,** p. 42.

At this point, the team has several possible choices of action:

- They can try to stay on the run, living in their vehicle, eating at Stuffer Shacks, and so on.
- They can find a hideout and try to jungle up, waiting out the opposition.
- They can confront Hernandez.
- They can, and probably will, combine aspects of these basic plans. For example, they may stay mobile while trying to learn more about the people who are after them, then find a safe spot to hide Maria and Max, then go after Hernandez.

If the team decides to set up a hideout, proceed to **Going To Ground,** p. 28.

If the team decides to find out about the price on their heads, go to **The Price Is Right,** p. 32. Use this section if they try to live on the run. It will warn them that this option leaves them too exposed.

If the team decides to go after Hernandez, proceed to **Hassling Hernandez,** p. 36. Be ready to roll some dice, because once the characters arrive at this section, events lead directly to the big fight with the yakuza in **Yakkity Yak.**

If the team decides to attempt to contact Hernandez for information, go to **Let's Talk It Over,** p. 34.

If a decker on the team made a deal with Max to rip off Hernandez's account at Federated Funds Net and decides to make that run now, a map of that system is included in **Fun At Federated,** p. 35.

BEHIND THE SCENES

Frankly, **Maria Mercurial** is written on the assumption that the shadowrunners will pick the option of finding and fortifying a hideout to use as a base of operations.

The gamemaster would find it useful to have the players map out their own home or homes before the adventure begins so that he will know the layout should they decide to hunker down in their own digs. Alternatively, they can use a trustworthy Contact to find a suitable location. Seattle is full of abandoned warehouses, empty tenements, office blocks, and so on that owners rent out to corps, shadowrunners, government agencies, and others for various covert uses. In certain neighborhoods, someone might as well put out a sign: "Abandoned Building Sites, Ltd. Ideal For Shadowrunners, Terrorists, Spies. Will Redesign To Suit. "

The cost of such a place is 500¥ per day, subject to negotiation. Have one character make an Opposed Negotiation Test against the landlord, with a Target Number 6. The landlord has a Negotiation Skill of 3. Every net success that a player achieves reduces the price by 50¥.

Note that if the shadowrunners do not pay the fee each day, the "landlord" simply puts out word of their whereabouts to the street. He would probably also turn them in for the reward. In such a case, Sumiko would know where they are hiding. She probably would not attack at once, but would watch their movements in and out of the hideout, waiting for the right moment. The Yakuza are most likely to strike whenever the place is least guarded.

This section includes a map of a typical "rent-a-hideout, " an abandoned warehouse that has been fixed up with living quarters.

There is also a map of Maria's luxury penthouse condo, in case the team decides to hole up there. Even if the condo does not end up as part of the adventure, it gives a good picture of what life can be like at the top of the heap in the Sixth World.

Let the shadowrunners rig up any kinds of alarms, booby traps, or other security they like. Anything that Max Foley knows about the team will get back to Sumiko if Max can find even five minutes away from observation by the others. (Unless someone follows him into the bathroom, this is pretty much a sure thing.) Max wants to make sure that his Shigeda "connection" stays informed so that she can protect him from Hernandez's goons if the team hoses things up. Outside of his knowledge of rock and roll, it appears that Max is none too bright.

The only thing that the runners will not be able to do is hire a lot of street muscle to assist them. As **The Price Is Right**, p. 32, shows, the lure of the big reward posted for finding Maria makes them a target for most of the other shadowrunners in town. A loyal buddy, fellow gang or tribe members, or followers (see **Shadowrun**, p. 53) are the only non-player characters the team can trust on this mission.

Once the hideout is set up, the shadowrunners can:
- Start checking the streets (**The Price Is Right**, p. 32).
- Try to contact Hernandez (**Let's Talk It Over**, p. 34).
- Deck into Federated Funds Net to nail the money Hernandez is holding out from Maria (**Fun At Federated**, p. 35).
- Go after Hernandez (**Hassling Hernandez**, p. 36).
- Or they can just sit tight, waiting out the five days of their agreement with Foley. If they take this stand, Sumiko will eventually come after them, having learned their whereabouts from Foley or from informants she has covering the city. See **Yakkity Yak**, p. 42, for this showdown.

DEBUGGING

A danger here is that the shadowrunners become fed up with Max and start to lean on him. There are some obvious holes in his story, and they may figure out that he is playing a double game.

Interrogating Max will be tricky, even if the characters use physical force. Someone would have to succeed at an Unresisted Interrogation Test to get him to admit his connection with the Shigeda and to tell Maria that the evidence against Hernandez was a frame-up. If the team simply questions Max, the Target Number is 11 (Max's Willpower +6). If they use physical persuasion, the Target Number is 8 (Max's Body +6).

The +6 is the same modifier in either case. The team may beat him up if they suspect he is playing fast and loose with them, but Max knows that Sumiko will kill him if he ruins her plan to get control of Maria's career.

Even if the shadowrunners get Max to talk, keep in mind that he does not know the real plan: to kidnap Maria and kill her. He thinks this whole scheme is simply a yakuza plot to get control of a major rocker and to recoup the money he owes them at the same time.

No matter what suspicions the shadowrunners have, the only proof of Hernandez's innocence that Maria will accept is a confession from Max about the frame-up. Any other evidence may make her suspicious or more willing to cooperate to find out the truth, but it will not weaken her resolve to break with Hernandez. Even if she is convinced of his innocence, Maria will be too ashamed to contact Hernandez, and the shadowrunners will have to act as go-betweens. This will, hopefully, get them over to his office, thus setting up the events in **Hassling Hernandez**, p. 36, that lead into the Yak attack in **Yakkity Yak**, p. 42.

RENT-A-HIDEOUT MAP KEY

This is a small warehouse in an abandoned industrial park out in the Barrens. It is about ten meters tall, but contains only a single story. All interior walls are Normal Construction Plastic (Barrier Rating 4). All windows have been paneled over with Thick Impact Plastic (Barrier Rating 10). All exterior doors have been replaced with a Reinforced Steel Sheet under a thin veneer (Barrier Rating 24). Locks are high-security, tooled steel. The Strength Test to break them (if the characters have a jimmy or crowbar) has a Target Number 15! Picking the locks has a Target Number 12 on the Success Test.

OFFICE SPACE (1)
STORAGE AREA (2)

This area is empty.

BATHROOM (3)
SMALL LOCKER ROOM (4)

Warehouse workers used this locker room when the place was in operation.

UNCLAIMED SHIPMENTS (5)

There is nothing of value here. The various stacks of boxes, crates, and drums are an average six meters high and sturdy enough to climb on. They count as Hard Cover. Knocking a section over requires an Unopposed Strength Test with a Target Number 12. Anyone hit by falling debris must resist 6M2 Stun damage.

MITSUBISHI JACKLIFT CARGO HANDLER
  Handling 2
  Speed 5/12
  Body 2
  Armor 0
  Signature 4
  Pilot 0

2044 MITSUBISHI JACKLIFT (6)

This Jacklift still functions and is equipped with both rigger inputs and manual controls. The Jacklift has both grappling arms and a forklift. The arms can be used to attack, using the vehicle skill for the Success Test. They have an effective Strength of 12, and can strike for 6M2 damage. All combat tests using the Jacklift are at +2 to the Target Numbers. After all, it was hardly designed for this sort of thing.

LOUNGE AREA (7)

This area has been modified to provide some minimal comforts for customers renting the building as a hideout. There is a battered trid unit and some cheap furniture. It is here that Sumiko offers the dreamchip to Maria in **Yakkity Yak**, p. 42.

FLIMSY SCREENS (8)

These provide Soft Cover only, and offer minimal privacy for several cots.

KITCHENETTE (9)

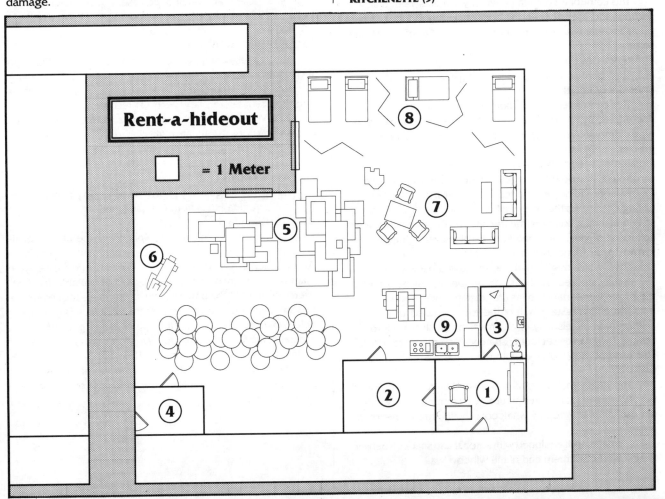

MARIA'S CONDO MAP KEY

Maria owns a penthouse condo on the 48th floor of Star Gardens Endominium, a high-security condominium building in downtown Seattle. The price tag was about 1. 5 million ¥. This is a typical Luxury Lifestyle establishment (see **Shadowrun**, p. 148).

All interior walls are Normal Impact Plastic or its equivalent (Barrier Rating 5). The ceiling is four meters high, with the overall ambiance light, spacious, and comfortable.

One thing the runners may notice (Intelligence Success Test with Target Number 5) is that the household controls all have keyboards or keypads attached. They have datajacks as well, but the characters will never see Maria jack in to operate anything. She *always* uses the manual controls. This is atypical in 2050. As usual, she brushes off direct questions about this behavior, saying simply that she prefers the "old-fashioned touch." In actuality, her datajack was wired so that its signals trigger the pleasure/pain centers of the brain. See **Maid in Japan**, p. 53, for the story on this. Maria does not jack into anything willingly except when she is synthlinking her music.

THE LANDING (1)

The building stairs, the passenger elevator, and a freight elevator all exit into this area.

CORRIDOR (2)

This corridor is scanned by security cameras, both building security and the tri-vid in the apartment can monitor. When Maria entertains, this area can be set up to hold a bar, buffet, and so on.

SPARE ROOM (3)

This room contains a closet to one side.

LIVING ROOM (4)

This centerpiece of the room is a large, circular conversation pit, revolving around a raised, open fireplace with a hood-type chimney over it. Maria is a strong supporter of ecological groups, and so she does not burn anything in the fireplace. It radiates infra-red heat and has a selection of holographic fires it can project, from low-burning coals to a cheery, snapping blaze.

A large vid screen (dotted lines) that rises from floor to ceiling dominates the north wall of the room. To the left of the screen stands a complex tri-vid console. The unit has a large collection of vids, trids, and sounds, plus every gimmick and gizmo to be found in a home entertainment center *except* simsense, which might strike the shadowrunners as odd.

A fully stocked autobar stands in the southwest corner of the room. Comfortable chairs are scattered here and there.

The entire eastern wall of the room consists of floor-to-ceiling glass panels, any or all of which can slide up into the ceiling. They can be set for transparency or dimmed to opacity. This window wall looks out onto the Garden, Area 5.

GARDEN (5)

This lovely rooftop garden is shaded by trees and dotted with flowerbeds and potted shrubs. A swimming pool occupies almost half of it. A roomy whirlpool is built into a corner of the area.

A smaller trid, equipped with autobar and snack dispenser, is against the southern end of the window wall.

KITCHEN (6)

This is a well-stocked kitchen, with deep-freeze, autorange, microwave, and all manner of cooking toys. Maria has a hired household staff most of the time, but when she is on her own, her tastes are simple. Large jars of peanut butter and grape jelly are standing out on a cutting board, along with a half-loaf of protobread.

UTILITY ROOM (7)

Here are located the circuit breakers, heating/AC unit, water heater, and so on.

FORMAL DINING ROOM (8)

A smaller breakfast nook, connected to the kitchen by a small serving hatch, is set up in the northern area of the room.

SMALL PARLOR (9)

For more intimate entertaining than the living room allows.

GUEST ROOM (10)

The bathroom is equipped with all the comforts, including a VibraSkrub sonic "shower. "

STORAGE ROOM (11)

Assorted odds and ends, cleaning supplies, and household servo units (automated vacuum cleaner, mopper, sweeper).

MARIA'S BEDROOM (12)

A very powerful trid unit is next to the bed. Several dressers line the walls. A small, tidy desk stands just inside the door, with a computer terminal on it. A concert quality Muzeeka 9000 Synthlink unit stands in the northeast corner of the room. Next to it, in a locked, air-conditioned case, is a beautiful acoustic guitar, a 1965 Martin, with rosewood inlays. It is worth at least 25, 000¥ on the collector's market.

RECORDING STUDIO (13)

This is a fully equipped recording studio, with all the high-tech tools available to the recording artist in 2050: synthlink interface, several top-of-the-line music generators, a Mitsuhama BandBox synthesizer, laser tech CD recorders, and a Konzert Acoustic Modulator, which can give this room acoustical qualities ranging from an intimate night club to a full-size concert hall. There is something like half-a-million nuyen worth of gear in here.

PRIVATE GARDEN (14)

This is Maria's getaway spot. It is laid out in Japanese style, but all the vegetation is from Central America.

GYMNASIUM (15)

This workout room is fully equipped with the latest Sendai-Nautilus Programmable Resistance equipment, PowerCycle Aerobic Station, Shiatsu-Matic massage unit, and a cyberware diagnostic and maintenance unit. A mat suitable for floor exercises, martial arts practice, and so on covers the floor in the western half of the room. Against the west wall is a complex holo-projector. This is a custom pistol range generator. In a cabinet at the far end of the room are stored several pistols that tie into the generator's computer. They "fire" safe laser pulses that the system will register. This little toy allows Maria to simulate numerous firearms practice scenarios from range fire to running gun battles.

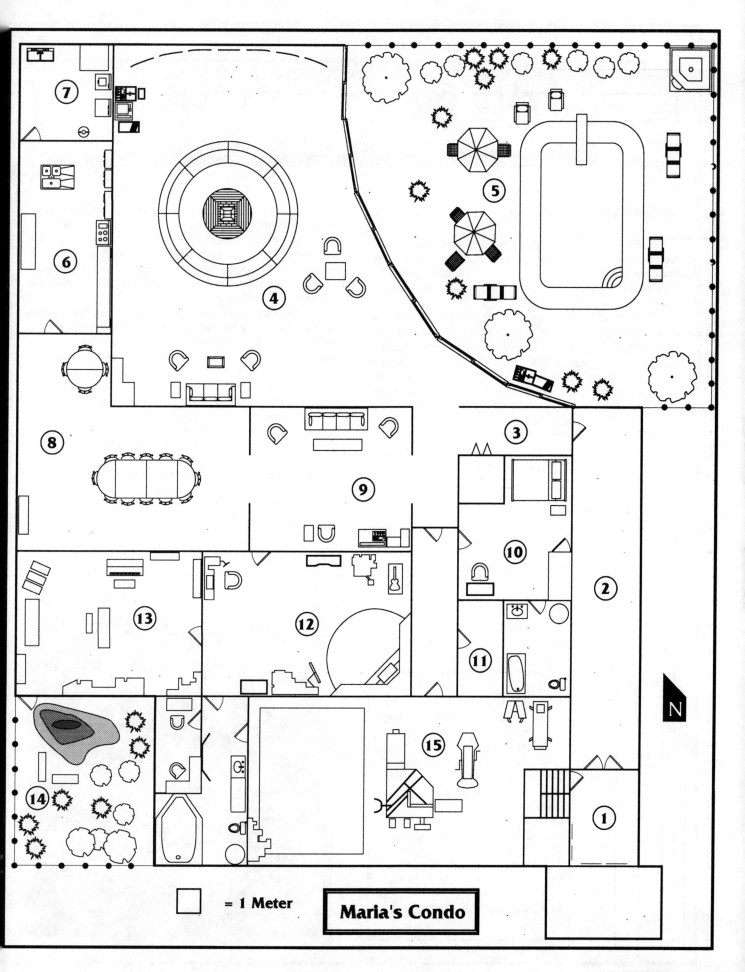

Maria's Condo

☐ = 1 Meter

N

BEHIND THE SCENES

This section comes into play if the team wants the word on the street. They have already been warned that they are hot, with person or persons unknown offering 10,000¥ for information on their whereabouts. They may wonder who wants to know.

Finding out requires the use of Etiquette (Street) Skill. A character must make an Unresisted Skill Test, with a Target Number 5. If using a personal Contact (e. g., Samurai, Shaman, Fixer), the Target Number is 4. If the characters use a very loyal Contact (a buddy or follower) as an informant, he gets the information without the need for a test, but the Contact also tells the character he has to split town on business. That Contact is unavailable for the rest of the adventure.

If several team members want to roll, no problem. Test each one separately. Any tests that succeed represent different Contacts. The team can follow up on any of them.

WORD ON THE STREET

0 Successes   No luck. Either no one wanted to talk, or the people the character contacted let their greed for the reward show enough that the shadowrunner was able to disengage before the other person could try to collect.

1–2 Successes   One or two successes means that a Contact is willing to talk, but wants to meet face-to-face. If the team refuses, the Contact will not give them any information. If the team accepts, the Contact gives them the same information as below, but also tries to collect the reward himself by setting up an ambush to occur after he leaves the meeting site.

3+ Successes   Three or more successes means the Contact tells what he knows: Word hit the street within an hour or two of the shootout at the Underworld that someone was willing to pay 10,000¥ for information on the whereabouts of either Maria or the shadowrunners. Anyone who could deliver one of the shadowrunners in condition to talk would get a bonus. Anyone with info to sell was to call 555-7395. That's all he knows.

If the Contact tries to collect the reward by setting up an ambush, set up the fight with two-to-one odds in favor of the ambushers, based on the number of shadowrunners the Contact *expected*. If the characters tell the Contact that two of them will attend the meet, four ambushers will be hiding at the site. If the other team members also cover the area, there will not be more ambushers waiting for them.

If the team suspects treachery or scouts out the site and observes the hiding ambushers, they can prevent the attack by some violent threat to their Contact. If they have him at gunpoint, for example, they can walk out of the meet without firing a shot.

The typical ambush will involve a bunch of street-gang members, hired by the treacherous Contact. Even if the gamemaster decides to create a different ambush, it should be easy for the characters to beat their opponents. This little scuffle is, after all, just a warm-up on the way to the main event.

The goal of this sequence is to create the right level of paranoia among the shadowrunners. If they take any kind of effective precautions against treachery, they should be able to withdraw from the meet without firing a shot. (Well, maybe a shot or two, but nothing heavy.)

STREET GANG MEMBERS

Use the Gang Member Archetype (**Shadowrun**, p. 39).

Armor:

Synth-leathers (Impact 1)

Weapons

For each pair of ambushers, one carries a Defiance T-250 Shotgun loading Stun Rounds (4M4 Stun Damage) and the other a Stun Baton. This weapon does 3L2 Stun Damage, based on the gang member's Strength. It also delivers an electric shock if it touches a target, with the results described in **Shadowrun**, p. 118. Disoriented characters add a +2 to all their Target Numbers.

Gang members also carry a Streetline Special (Damage 3L1), the usual firearm for the Archetype.

The gang members want to take at least one prisoner. The shadowrunners are not worth anything to them dead. If they are losing badly, obviously outnumbered, or ambushed in their turn, the gangers will run rather than fight. Of course, if the shadowrunners prevent them from running, the gangers will fight to kill. The gang members are open about this, with members obviously backing off, yelling obscene requests for mercy ("Hey, it's sub-zero, fragger! I'm outta here, O. K.?") Make it clear to the players when an opponent is ready to quit. If they still want to press the matter, so be it.

Whether the team had to fight for the information or not, the comm code they got is the real one. If they decide to call it, proceed to **Let's Talk It Over**, the next section.

DEBUGGING

If the shadowrunners decide to waltz out onto the street, innocently asking the denizens of Seattle's nightside if they have heard anything about a reward, they are going to get sliced up for lunch meat. This is a case where the gamemaster can simply point out to the players that their characters would not be quite so naive. "Hey, chummers, someone with nuyen to burn is advertising for your heads. There are slicers out there who'd geek their own mothers for 10¥, much less 10,000¥!"

On the other hand, if the team simply swaggers around armed to the teeth, daring the street to do its worst, go ahead and oblige them. As a warning shot, a gang of a dozen or so punks like the ones described above might come after them. If beating those kinds of odds makes the player characters overconfident, send a couple of street samurai after them (use the Archetype, **Shadowrun** p. 46). Anytime a team member goes out to the store, half a dozen toughies will track him, drooling for the reward. They may not get up their nerve to attack this time, but eventually they will try it.

The goal is to maneuver the shadowrunners into a hideout. If they decide to stay on the run, dodging half the goons in Seattle, they will be hunted every moment.

If the shadowrunners win two or three of these encounters and the adventure seems stalled, then Sumiko will make the potentially fatal mistake of losing patience, and come after them with her yakuza team. Proceed to **Yakkity Yak**, p. 42, for the big fight. If the team always keeps Maria with them, the yak will strike in the most isolated spot they can, using periodic feeds of information from Max Foley to figure out where they can catch the team off guard, or at least out in the open. Ideally, the yakuza will try to strike when Maria is not guarded by the entire team of shadowrunners.

LET'S TALK IT OVER

BEHIND THE SCENES

This section can go one of two ways, or even both ways.

If the shadowrunners look up the phone number for Armando Hernandez in the Seattle Directory Assistance Database, they will find it listed as 555-7395. That, you may recall, is also the number they received for information about Maria or her associates.

If they ask Maria for Armando's number, she tells them it is 555-9845.

If they call 555-7395, a sultry, gorgeous redhead answers. If the callers are not using a phone equipped with a vidscreen, they will still be impressed by the husky, sexy voice of Hernandez's secretary.

If the callers ask for Hernandez, she answers:

"I'm sorry. Mr. Hernandez is out of town this week. May someone else help you?"

If the callers claim to be a band wanting an audition:

"Oh, that would be fine. The studio is booked until the end of the month, but we can make an appointment for about two weeks from now. If you tell me your address, I can send you our guidelines. "

If the callers refer to Maria or the reward:

"You need to speak to Ms. Sakura, our Talent Contract Manager. Let me connect you. " The line goes on hold for a moment, then rings.

It is answered by an attractive, Japanese woman in her mid-thirties. She wears a severe dark business suit and a few pieces of elegant, simple jewelry. Her hair and makeup are trendy in the understated way that is the height of fashion among corporate women. "This is Kathy Sakura. I believe you have some information for me. "

The speaker is, in fact, Sumiko Hotoda. If the magician can see her now and had assensed her appearance in the fight with the Street Samurai at Underworld 93 (see **It's Shootout Time**, p. 20.), he will recognize her as the mage. In any case, if any magicians are able to see "Kathy Sakura, " make a secret Unresisted Sorcery Test with a Target Number 4.

On one or two successes, the magician will notice that the design of her elegant jewelry uses occult symbols. That is common enough, though.

With three or four successes, the magician will notice that the jewelry uses absolutely correct magical symbolism, which suggests that they might be focuses.

More successes verify that at least one piece of jewelry looks like a working focus, though there is no way to assense its power over a phone.

For other details on Sumiko Hotoda, see her character description in **Yakkity Yak**, p. 43.

Ms. Sakura will be very pleased at any information the shadowrunners can give her about Ms. Mercurial. "Our legal department is very concerned at her actions and we intend to pursue the matter in court, " she says. "In the meantime, we would hate to see her jeopardize her career in any way. Of course, anyone impeding our efforts to contact Ms. Mercurial would also be subject to litigation, but we are prepared to pay customary finder's fees to anyone who assists us. "

She will readily agree to pay up to double the original offer—20,000¥!—for useful information. She will also agree to any meeting the team proposes, as she has not the slightest intention of showing up. Even if she does not recognize the callers as her opponents, she is sure that either Foley or her own agents will soon track down the prey. Therefore, she has decided to stall anyone calling to get the reward.

She will deny any knowledge of attacks upon Maria or the shadowrunners, and suggests that such allegations are subject to slander suits.

If Maria sees the call take place, or the team tells her about it, she will be puzzled. She tells them that Hernandez has no sexy redheaded secretary, and no one named Kathy Sakura works for him. In fact, Hernandez works alone, hiring temps as needed for particular jobs. His office routine, like most people's, depends on his computer system. Maria is especially puzzled about the phone number. Armando's number is 555-9845! The yakuza bribed a phone company worker to slip a false number into the directory, so that they could intercept at least some of Hernandez's phone calls.

If the shadowrunners call 555-9845, they get a recording with music playing in the background. Not surprisingly, it is a Mercurial song, her first hit, "Who Weeps For The Children?" If the callers are using a vidphone, it displays a montage of images from her tour last year. If Maria is present, this proves too much for her, and she runs out of the room or away from the booth, depending on the surroundings. The main thing is she goes AWAY!

The recording is of a man's voice, with an Aztlan accent:

"Hello, this is Armando Hernandez. Sorry, friends, but I'm on the road until next week. Please leave a message. To zip me a demo, hit the transmit key now. Adios. " The unit beeps, ready to receive a message.

If the players leave a message that mentions Maria, the answering machine will go off-line and Hernandez comes on, asking them to come to his office. If they refuse, he pleads desperately to meet at any time or place of their choosing. He wants to talk to them and will be totally cooperative.

If the team agrees to a meet, they get the information described in **Hassling Hernandez**, p. 36.

FUN AT FEDERATED

BEHIND THE SCENES

Foley gave the decker Federated's system address so that he could jump straight to their SAN and get into it. This is a little system, what decker slang would call a "piggy bank, " but even small systems can burn an overconfident decker.

This is where Federated stores its account information. Each account file is protected with Scramble 3. Failure to unscramble successfully dumps the file off-line. This has the effect of blocking the depositor's access to his funds until the account is restored.

If the decker is here to steal Armando's account, he will see that it is the only one currently in the system that is worth more than a few hundred nuyen. This is a dinky little system, after all.

Hernandez's file is 90 Mp in size and worth 180, 000¥. Size does not matter if the decker transfers it to Foley's bank, as arranged. He just tells the Federated Funds Net computer to make the transfer and, bingo, the file vanishes. This is a system operation, which means the decker must pass an Unresisted Computer Skill Test with a Target Number 3. Because this is a Red Node, he must score at least three successes.

If the decker decides to steal the account for himself, he must defeat the Scramble Ice and download the file, as described in **Shadowrun**, p. 102.

If the decker is there to investigate Hernandez's missing account, he finds an empty file under the agent's account number. He can look for clues, making an Unresisted Computer Skill Test with a Target Number 4. He must make at least three successes to get any information, because this is a Red Node. If the test succeeds, he will observe subtle indications that the decker who ripped the file is the same one who invaded Armando's office computer.

If Federated's system goes into External Alert, the operator immediately starts a shutdown (2D6 turns warning to the decker). A marginal operation like Federated Funds Net cannot afford to keep deckers on retainer to defend their system.

FEDERATED FUNDS NET MAP KEY

NODE 1
Orange-3 SAN. Access 4.
NODE 2
Green-3 SPU. Barrier 3.
NODE 3
Red-3 Datastore. Trace and Dump 5.
NODE 4
Orange-4 CPU. Killer 4. The Hernandez file transfer can be made from here as well.

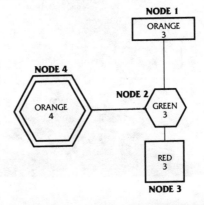

TELL IT TO THEM STRAIGHT

GAMEMASTER'S NOTE: If the shadowrunners break into Hernandez's place, they find him asleep on the sofa in his private office. An empty tequila bottle is lying on the floor next to him. If they wake him, he is passive at first and treats them as robbers. "There's not much here, but take what you want. It doesn't matter anymore."

If they mention Maria, he demands to know where she is. If he believes that they are working on her behalf or if they ask about the breakup between them, read the following text to them.

Of course, if Hernandez is expecting the team, whether in his office or at some neutral site, then simply read the following to the shadowrunners straight-away.

Hernandez looks at you with a kind of quiet desperation. His eyes are bloodshot, and it is apparent that he's been drinking, but when he talks about Maria, it seems to steady him. He says he does not know why she went over to Foley. She has refused to return any of his calls.

He grows melancholy and begins to muse about his early relationship with Maria.

"I emigrated from Aztlan in the twenties. I have lived in Seattle since then, for it is a city where the children with the dreams, the dreams that make strong music, often come.

"Five years ago, I was in the *barranca*, the Barrens. Lots of new bands play the little clubs there, you know? A *chico* offered me the usual kinds of entertainment. I was about to tell him to buzz when he pulls out a cheap player and wants to show me what he can offer. On the screen was a beautiful girl—a child, really, her limbs silvered like a mirror—and she was singing. It was Maria, of course. She was singing a *cantamuerte*. Do you know the *cantamuerte, señores*? Street music from Aztlan, born of the *indio* chants. Gang members often sing it before they fight to the death.

"That idiot pimp didn't understand. He was offering me the body on the screen, but it was the voice that I wanted. I went with him, and ended up killing him to get Maria out of that cheap brothel. They had her addicted to some dreamchips so they could force her to trick for them. It affected her memory. She has never been able to recall how she came to be there or who had her modified with the silver skin.

"I got her medical help to kick the BTLs. Then we began to build her career. She will be one of the great ones, whether it is I who represents her or even a *hijo de puta* like Max Foley. All I want is to know why she is angry with me."

BEHIND THE SCENES

Well, by now, the shadowrunners may begin to suspect that things are not as they have been told. If Hernandez is telling the truth, it seems likely that he was framed.

If they tell him about the "evidence" Maria found, he will explode in a furious denial. The system crash Maria mentioned was, he is pretty sure, caused by a decker. He thought nothing of it at the time, assumed it was some vandal randomly breaking into the system. He bought some tougher Ice for his SAN, restored most of the lost data, and forgot about it. After all, there is nothing on his office system that anyone would want to steal. It never occurred to him that someone might be planting data on the computer.

He tells the team that he has since learned to be more careful. He has just discovered that someone busted into his Federated Funds Net account and totally wiped out his savings. If the shadowrunners did, in fact, rip off Hernandez's account, they can tell him if they wish. If they *didn't* do it, this is a clue that someone else has a decker working on this case.

Examining Hernandez's office system will provide some clues, if anyone thinks of doing it. He will give the team his passcodes, so they can access his office computer freely. They can either use a terminal, or a decker can access it via the Matrix. No system map is provided, because in either case, the team will have full access to the computer.

Have a character make an Unresisted Computer Skill Test with a Target Number 5 if using a terminal, or a 4 if decking. The more successes the decker rolls, the more information he gets. Additional tests to increase the total number of successes are allowed. That is, if he gets four successes on the first test, and two on the second, give him any information that requires six successes or less. Each test made after the first increases the Target Number by +2.

ACCESSING THE SYSTEM

1 Success	The character can tell that the system crash a few weeks ago was caused by a decker invading the system.
2 Successes	The decker was not very good. He left traces of his operation all over the place, little fingerprints in the Matrix, for example. If the character ever comes across his work again, he'll probably recognize it.
3 Successes	The character finds some fragments of the datafiles that Maria erased, the ones implicating Hernandez in pushing BTL chips. It is hard to get much sense out of them.
4–5 Successes	The character can reconstruct the fragments. They list payments and records "proving" Hernandez was a front for the Shigeda syndicate, moving dreamchips into the rock trade. Any Seattle shadowrunner will know about the Shigeda, especially that it is not a good idea to mess with them!
6+ Successes	The character finds some broken data trails showing where someone pried out the access code for Armando's account at Federated Funds Net.

At this point, there are several things the team might do:
- If they simply head back to their hideout, they will walk straight into the yakuza, who have hit it while they were out. Go to **Yakkity Yak**, p. 42.
- If they try to call the hideout, they get no answer. **Yakkity Yak** still covers the fighting, but the team can try a soft entry if they suspect trouble.
- The team might decide that they should see what is in Max Foley's computer. After all, he gave them his system address so they could pull off the run on Funds Net and shoot him the loot. The gamemaster can remind the players if they have forgotten. If the shadowrunners decide to send a decker into Max's computer, proceed to **Decking Foley**, p. 39.

If the team decides to do anything else, such as legwork on the streets or investigating Foley's office, they will not find much going on. The fight with the yakuza will take place when they get back to wherever they have stashed Maria.

Hernandez will try to persuade the shadowrunners to take him to wherever Maria is. If he hears about yakuza attacks or anything else that makes him think Maria is in danger, he will grab his weapon and *demand* that they take him with them. The only way the shadowrunners can stop him is by knocking him cold.

DEBUGGING

The worst-case goof the shadowrunners can pull here is to kill Hernandez. By now, they should be catching on that this guy loves Maria, at least like a father, and perhaps in a more passionate sense as well. The evidence that he is a fall guy in some Nefarious Plot is getting pretty overwhelming. Of course, they may decide that their contract requires them to kill him, but the gamemaster can point out that the deal is to *protect Maria!* If Hernandez is not a threat to her, and in fact may be the only guy apart from the shadowrunners themselves who is actively concerned for her welfare, then geeking him may not be the most appropriate course. Point this out to the team if they seem on the verge of something rash.

If they do kill Hernandez, it is a tragic error, but will not materially affect the rest of the story. Maria will, of course, become an implacable enemy once she learns the whole truth. This can provide the basis for some pretty hair-raising future adventures, as the rightfully vengeful Ms. Mercurial goes after the people who killed her dearest friend. A glance at Maria's statistics will show that she is not an enemy to be taken lightly. Add the resources of her wealth and influence, and the shadowrunners may wish they had been a little less quick to go for the kill.

Another serious error that will require no debugging (at least not yet) is if the team casually wanders on back to their hideout without taking any precautions, walking straight into a yakuza ambush. If they have taken any precautions at all (subtle signals to indicate an intrusion, leaving a guard outside the hideout, and so on), then reward their foresight by letting them know that something is amiss. The action then proceeds as described in **Yakkity Yak**, p. 42.

ARMANDO HERNANDEZ'S OFFICE MAP KEY

Armando lives and works in an old brownstone in a "gentrified" area of downtown Seattle, one that has largely escaped the urban makeovers of the past century. The first floor is devoted to his office and a well-equipped recording studio. His living quarters are on the second floor.

WAITING ROOM (1)
ARMANDO'S OFFICE (2)

His office computer system is installed here next to a messy desk against the west wall. In the north wall, a pane of glass looks into the recording studio (Room #3). In front of this window is a complex control panel. Several bookshelves filled with magazines, technical manuals for recording equipment, and even some hardback fiction (antiques!) line the other two walls.

Pictures of Maria hang everywhere.

If the shadowrunners are sneaking into the office, they will find Hernandez sleeping on the couch in this room.

RECORDING STUDIO (3)

This room is equipped with the latest and best in recording technology.

LIBRARY (4)

This room is lined with bookshelves, containing thousands of volumes. Hernandez seems to have a taste for antique media. A trid sits in one corner. On the desk against the south wall is a terminal hooked into the office computer. A comfortable chair sits in the middle of the room. On a table next to it, open face-down, is a copy of *Don Quixote*, in the original Spanish. If anyone can read it, it is open to the chapter where Quixote first meets Dulcinea.

HERNANDEZ'S BEDROOM (5)

A picture of Maria sits on the table next to the bed.

KITCHEN (6)
DINING ROOM (7)
SPARE BEDROOM (8)

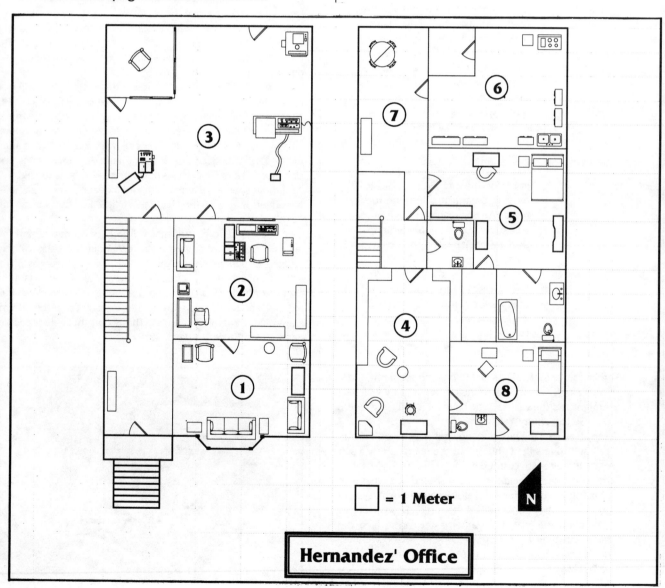

= 1 Meter

N

Hernandez' Office

DECKING FOLEY

TELL IT TO THEM STRAIGHT

You punch in the coordinates for Foley's system and hit the power switch on your cyberdeck. The world dissolves into a glittering swirl of flashing phosphor-patterns as the simsense circuitry takes over your vision, then the glittering vistas of the Matrix unfold around you. Welcome home, decker.

You flash up to Foley's SAN, piggybacking on a mass-distribution tele-sales message. As you slip into the access node, you see a shimmering mass of ice in the way. A quick scan makes your eyes widen. What is a two-bit fixer like Max Foley doing with such hot ice on his phone line, for Ghost's sake? If the access port is guarded this way, what has he got waiting for you inside? This little picnic just picked up some very nasty-looking ants.

Choosing your first utility, you sleaze toward the glittering barrier of anti-intrusion code, and then…

BEHIND THE SCENES

What happens next depends on the decker.

Strictly speaking, he should not get a warning that things are not what they seem. But what the heck, the decker is going to have enough trouble, so a little hint that Max's system is loaded for bear is not entirely out of line.

If an external alert is triggered, the decker is going to find out who has been doing all those runs for Max. Gum E. Bear, the decker Max hired to slip the "evidence" into Hernandez's system, is on watch. He has all Max's passcodes and will attack the invading decker. If Bear is defeated, he will initiate a system shutdown once he comes out of dump-shock.

DEBUGGING

If the team decks Foley's machine without leaving their hideout, then they have learned of Max's double-dealing and the imminent yakuza attack in the nick of time.

Literally at the same moment that the decker reads Hotoda's message (Node 4), any sentries should report several sleek black vans pulling up outside the hideout. Proceed at once to **Yakkity Yak**. Give the team about one minute to set up and start the fight.

GUM E. BEAR

Bear is just hired help. If he loses sight of the opposing decker or is taking too much of a beating, he will not go to great lengths to protect Max's system. He will jack out and start the shutdown. He is not getting paid enough to worry about what the invader might do in the time it takes the system to wind down.

Attributes
    Body: 2
    Quickness: 4
    Strength: 3
    Charisma: 3
    Intelligence: 4
    Willpower: 3
    Essence: 5.8
    Reaction: 4 (6 in the Matrix)
Skills:
    Decking: 6
Dice Pools:
    Dodge: 4
    Hacking: 12
Cyberware:
    Fuchi DATA JACK Cyber-7 with Level 1 Response Increase (see **Shadowrun**, p. 105).
        Programs:
        Bod: 5
        Evasion: 4
        Masking: 4
        Sensors: 6
        Attack: 6
        Medic: 8
        Shield: 3

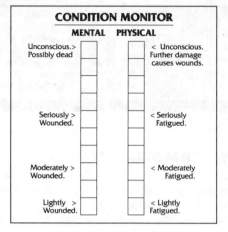

CONDITION MONITOR

MENTAL	PHYSICAL
Unconscious.> Possibly dead	< Unconscious. Further damage causes wounds.
Seriously > Wounded.	< Seriously Fatigued.
Moderately > Wounded.	< Moderately Fatigued.
Lightly > Wounded.	< Lightly Fatigued.

CONDITION MONITOR

MENTAL	PHYSICAL
Unconscious.> Possibly dead	< Unconscious. Further damage causes wounds.
Seriously > Wounded.	< Seriously Fatigued.
Moderately > Wounded.	< Moderately Fatigued.
Lightly > Wounded.	< Lightly Fatigued.

FOLEY SYSTEM MAP KEY

NODE 1

SAN. Orange-4 running Trapped Access 4. Gray IC is Killer 5. This cost Max quite a bundle, but he got nervous seeing how easily Hernandez got ripped by his own decker. A guy can't be too careful. I mean, data is all you got nowadays, am I right?

NODE 2

SPU. Green-5 running Barrier 3.

NODE 3

Datastore. Green-3. No IC. This is public correspondence, tax figures (the ones Max puts on his income tax form), publicity material on his acts, and so forth. Nothing of value. Browsing for references to Maria, Hernandez, or others will reveal nothing but what could be obtained from watching the news on tri-vid.

NODE 4

Blue-4. A cluster of Slave Modules. These are the computer's interface to the recording gear, office machinery, answering machine, apartment gadgetry, and so on.

If the decker investigates the answering machine, he will find one message on it. He can play it back, as it is a system operation. He will see a Japanese woman, who delivers the following message:

"Foley, I don't know if you'll see this in time or not. Time is running out. Try to keep your watchdogs calm. I have received warning that Hernandez is about to attack. You need my protection. I know your location and will be there in a few minutes. Whatever you do, keep the woman with you. Don't fail me, Foley. The Shigeda have little use for incompetent people."

If the decker saw "Kathy Sakura" in **Let's Talk It Over**, p. 34, he will recognize her as the speaker. However, instead of elegant business clothes, she is in street armor, and behind her are shadowy figures readying their weapons for combat.

The timestamp on this message shows it came in about half an hour ago. Presumably, the team will realize their hideout is under attack and zoom back there. Note that it is *too late* to warn anybody who stayed behind to guard Maria. Their fight with the yakuza has already happened. Proceed at once to **Yakkity Yak**, p. 42, to resolve any combat.

NODE 5

Orange-5. Datastore. Trace and Dump 4. This is Max's private file space. Among the items found here are an 80 Mp file locked with Scramble 4. This contains Max's real earning statements. Though this data has no cash value, if downloaded, it will permit the team to blackmail Max, whose tax returns bear little resemblance to the income recorded in this file. Reading this file also reveals that Max is about half-a-million nuyen in the hole to a loan shark named Toroshi. Anyone with Etiquette (Street) Skill knows Toroshi is well connected to a yakuza gang. Passing an Unresisted Etiquette (Street) Test with a Target Number 5 reveals that Toroshi is, in fact, connected to the Shigeda.

Max's private file also contains a coded bank account interface, protected by Scramble 4. If the character can open this, he can dump Max's account into his own. 180,000¥ of that is Hernandez's. That must mean the other 120,000¥ belongs to Foley. A system operation (Unresisted Computer Skill Test, Target Number 5, requiring two successes) lets the character transfer any or all of the money into Hernandez's account. If the character dumps any of the funds into one of his own accounts or downloads the credit himself (treat it as a size 50 Mp file), he must launder it, unless he also has a means of keeping Max from reporting the theft (blackmail using the tax file, physical threats, and so forth).

Also in Foley's private file is an unguarded 20 Mp datafile. Reading it, the character can see that it is Max's private diary. Most of the entries deal with his business, but there are several that mix business with Max's dubious ideas of pleasure.

Examining the data for the past few weeks, the character sees an entry that says: "Mrs. Foley's little boy is saved. Toroshi says the Shigeda have a deal to settle that little financial problem of mine. On top of that, I get control of Mercurial and stick it to that fraggin' Hernandez. Is this a great country, or what?" It is dated the same day that Maria discovered the planted evidence that incriminated Hernandez.

NODE 6

SPU. Green-5. Running Barrier 5.

NODE 7

The CPU. Orange-3. No IC.

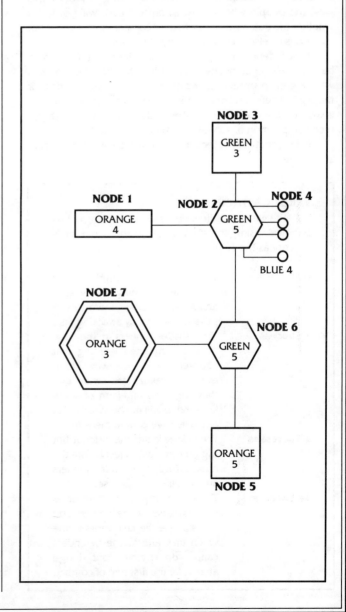

YAKKITY YAK

BEHIND THE SCENES

If any *player* characters are guarding Maria, they must deal with the yakuza attack without help from their teammates who are visiting Hernandez. As soon as the characters visiting Hernandez realize that the yakuza are attacking their base, or indeed, that they have already attacked, play out the invasion of the site by Hotoda and her soldiers. The gamemaster may wish to ask players not involved in this fight to leave the room, or conversely, take the players involved into another room. This way, the people who are away from the base will not know whether the outcome will leave their companions battered but victorious or else the yakuza firmly in control.

If the hideout has any security, assign it a rating. This should be the Intelligence of any live sentries, the skill of the person who rigged up any automated defenses, or perhaps a rating for the type of defense. For example, a video-only camera system is worth 4; a sound-sensor or IR beam system is worth 5; a high-tech combination of surveillance systems is worth 6.

If different types of security are installed, use the best score among them.

YAKUZA ATTACK

The yakuza soldiers all have Stealth Rating 6. Roll six dice, using the number assigned to the site's security as the Target.

0 Successes	The shadowrunners at the base have one minute's warning of the yakuza attack, which allows them to surprise the yakuza by attacking first.
1 Success	The shadowrunners at the base have one minute's warning that attackers are on the way. However, the yakuza are aware that they triggered an alarm of some kind and so will not be surprised at any defensive countermeasures.
2 Successes	The yakuza enter the hideout but trigger some alarm just before the attack. Thus, the shadowrunners are not taken by surprise.
3+ Successes	The yakuza can position themselves in any way within the hideout, and will surprise the characters inside when they attack. The defenders cannot do anything but dodge attacks for the first turn of combat.

If there are no *player* characters guarding Maria:

It does not matter if they have left Godzilla to guard the place. Any non-player character allies left on their own in the hideout will be disabled, captured, or killed when the yakuza attack. When the player characters get back, go to **Down to the Wire,** p. 45.

If they have one or more player characters with them:

They fight normally. Let the players involved run the NPCs any way they wish in combat, but note that only a follower will risk death for a player character. As stated on **Shadowrun**, p. 53, a follower is willing die for you. Any other character who is confronted with overwhelming odds or seriously wounded will probably surrender or run. Surrender is unwise; the Shigeda are not interested in leaving witnesses. To avoid unnecessary losses, they will take prisoners during the fight. Time enough to kill them after securing the prize.

If the defenders kill the yakuza:

Part One of the adventure is over. Hotoda attempts to escape if the fight is going against her soldiers, though they will fight to the death. Proceed to **Boy, I'm Glad That's Over,** p. 46.

If the yakuza capture the hideout:

The characters who were away will return to find the scene described in **Down to the Wire,** p. 45. If they were expecting trouble, they will sneak into the hideout area. If they just come sauntering in, the yakuza will ambush them. Arrange the yak into the best positions possible for such an ambush (plenty of cover, overlapping lines of fire, and so on). Conclude this fight and then go to **Down to the Wire** if the yakuza win, or to **Boy, I'm Glad That's Over** if the shadowrunners win.

DEBUGGING

If all the shadowrunners are guarding the hideout, fortressed up, never leaving, Sumiko will have to risk an all-out attack. Remember that unless they have discovered his activity, Max is keeping her posted of the situation at the hideout: how many people are there, when they go out, where they are going (if he knows), and so on. If the team gets a hold on Max, they can always turn this to their advantage, setting a trap for the yakuza.

If Sumiko kills or incapacitates all the shadowrunners, she will take off with Maria. This ends Part One of the adventure. If the gamemaster wants to let another team of runners attempt to save the Quicksilver Queen, Hernandez can survive the debacle, and bring them in to pick up Part Two.

SUMIKO HOTODA

Sumiko is a mage and a mid-level *kobun* or member of the Shigeda-*gumi*, the Shigeda syndicate, a powerful gang of yakuza operating in Seattle. She is a pure-blood Japanese, in her late thirties, and very attractive. She was trained by a major corp in Japan before becoming fed up with the ingrained sexism of the traditional *zaibatsu* structure, and emigrating to Seattle, where she established contacts with the underworld. The Shigeda rewarded her performance of various missions with increased perquisites, and she formally entered the gang four years ago. She is equally at home at a cut-throat boardroom meeting or on the midst of a throat-cutting gang fight in an alley. She can be the very image of subdued, oriental femininity one minute and all cold-blooded efficiency the next.

Sumiko has no foolish notions of honor or courage. She leads her soldiers from the rear, prefers to shoot from ambush, and adheres to the yakuza code only so far as it is part of her obligation to the Shigeda. She will kill, without hesitation, anyone who is in her way. If the shadowrunners give her any opportunity to damage them, she will take it.

Attributes:
- Body: 3
- Quickness: 3
- Strength: 3
- Charisma: 5
- Intelligence: 6
- Willpower: 5
- Essence: 6
- Magic: 5(7)**
- Reaction: 5(9)*

Skills:
- Conjuring: 4
- Firearms: 6
- Monofilament Whip: 5
- Unarmed Combat: 5
- Sorcery: 7

Special Skills
- Karate: 6

*Sumiko's Reaction is enhanced +2 by the Increase Reaction Spell. This also gives her *three Initiative dice!* She wears a Spell Lock to permanently hold the spell on herself. It imposes no Distractions on her and so does not count against her when casting Exclusive Spells.

**With Power Focus active

Dice Pools:
- Astral: 18
- Defense (Armed): 4
- Defense (Unarmed): 6
- Dodge: 3
- Magic: 7

Cyberware:
None

Gear:
- Ares Predator loading Explosive Rounds (2 reloads) and Laser Sight (–1 to Target Number to hit)
- Armor Jacket (Ballistic 5, Impact 3)
- Staff (Power Focus Rating +2)
- Medallion (Spell Focus for Ignite with +2 rating)
- Monofilament Whip

Spells:

Combat:
- Mana Bolt: 7
- Sleep: 6

Detection:
- Analyze Truth: 4
- Detect Enemies: 6

Health:
- Increase Reaction: +2–+5
- Heal Severe Wounds: 5

Manipulation:
- Barrier: 7
- Ignite: 6

CONDITION MONITOR		
MENTAL	**PHYSICAL**	
Unconscious.> Possibly dead		< Unconscious. Further damage causes wounds.
Seriously > Wounded.		< Seriously Fatigued.
Moderately > Wounded.		< Moderately Fatigued.
Lightly > Wounded.		< Lightly Fatigued.

YAKUZA SOLDIERS

The number of soldiers Sumiko has with her equals the number of characters opposing her in the final shootout, minus one. The "minus one" is lying in front of Maria with his face blown off.

If there are player characters opposing the initial invasion of the hideout, the more soldiers they can knock off before succumbing, the fewer their companions will have to face. Sumiko cannot call in reinforcements.

During a fight, the soldiers will tend to work in pairs, each pair concentrating their attacks on one target at a time. The soldiers have no qualms about charging a gunman with their swords out, if they think they can withstand a shot while getting into katana range.

The soldiers will die to protect Sumiko and have been ordered to die rather than kill Maria. They will fight her with sheathed swords (doing Stun damage) or bare-handed, rather than shooting or slashing her.

Attributes:
Body: 4
Quickness: 4(6)*
Strength: 5(7)*
Charisma: 2
Intelligence: 3
Willpower: 3
Essence: 2
Reaction: 4(6)**

Skills:
Armed Combat: 6
Firearms: 4
Stealth: 6
Unarmed Combat: 6

*Strength and Quickness enhanced by Muscle Replacement.
**Reaction increased by +2 due to Wired Reflexes. Note that the soldiers have 2D6 for Initiative.

Dice Pools:
Defense (Armed): 6
Defense (Unarmed): 6
Dodge: 6

Cyberware:
Muscle Replacement: 2
Wired Reflexes: 1

Gear:
Armor jacket (Ballistic 5, Impact 3)
Concussion Grenades (2)
Heckler & Koch HK227 (2 extra clips) with Laser Sight and Silencer
Katana

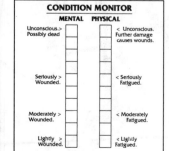

CONDITION MONITOR

	MENTAL	PHYSICAL	
Unconscious.> Possibly dead			< Unconscious. Further damage causes wounds.
Seriously > Wounded.			< Seriously Fatigued.
Moderately > Wounded.			< Moderately Fatigued.
Lightly > Wounded.			< Lightly Fatigued.

CONDITION MONITOR

	MENTAL	PHYSICAL	
Unconscious.> Possibly dead			< Unconscious. Further damage causes wounds.
Seriously > Wounded.			< Seriously Fatigued.
Moderately > Wounded.			< Moderately Fatigued.
Lightly > Wounded.			< Lightly Fatigued.

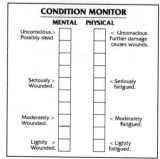

CONDITION MONITOR

	MENTAL	PHYSICAL	
Unconscious.> Possibly dead			< Unconscious. Further damage causes wounds.
Seriously > Wounded.			< Seriously Fatigued.
Moderately > Wounded.			< Moderately Fatigued.
Lightly > Wounded.			< Lightly Fatigued.

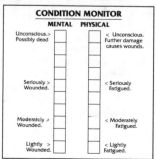

CONDITION MONITOR

	MENTAL	PHYSICAL	
Unconscious.> Possibly dead			< Unconscious. Further damage causes wounds.
Seriously > Wounded.			< Seriously Fatigued.
Moderately > Wounded.			< Moderately Fatigued.
Lightly > Wounded.			< Lightly Fatigued.

DOWN TO THE WIRE

TELL IT TO THEM STRAIGHT

You see Maria, backed into a corner by half-a-dozen armed and armored opponents. They are keeping her at bay with sheathed katana, or telescoping bo-staffs. One of them is sprawled at her feet, the top of his head blown off. Maria is holding her Browning Max-Power in front of her, the slide locked back, empty. Her eyes are locked on the woman who stands behind the line of warriors. Human eyes, staring out of her silver face, locked on the woman as if she were holding Maria's soul out to her.

"Kathy Sakura" is about two meters away from Maria. She holds an ornate walking stick tucked under one arm. Her other hand is extended toward Maria, offering her something…something that *buzzes* softly. You recognize it as a modified simsense unit, the kind used by chip-heads. Dreamchippers.

"You see, my dear, you're with friends. Don't try to fight us. See what I have here for you? Isn't that pretty music it makes? You've missed it, haven't you? Now, just stop all this foolishness and it's all yours. "

BEHIND THE SCENES

The tableau holds until the shadowrunners make their move. When they attack, Sumiko utters a curse and drops the BTL unit as she dives for cover. It bounces and skitters across the floor, eventually landing in front of Maria, like a malignant pet wanting to play. Slowly, she sinks to her knees, staring down at the unit, hypnotized. In five turns, she will jack it in. Once re-addicted to BTLs, the odds of her retaining any shred of sanity are pretty low. This is no problem for Hotoda and Morgan, since they can retrieve the sealed memory from a drooling chiphead as easily as from a sane woman.

With this development, the shadowrunners must not only defeat the yakuza but they must also try to get the dreamchip unit away from Maria. If she jacks the chip, she will fall unconscious. The yak can easily scoop her up and fight their way out, and will try to do so if this happens. Sumiko and one soldier will grab the unconscious singer and attempt a getaway, with the remaining soldiers trying to pin down the shadowrunners. Once outside, Maria will be picked up by Perianwyr (remember the Dragon?), who will carry her to the Taetzel Building. Peri will first flame Sumiko and her soldier, thus neatly tying up that particular loose end. Proceed to **The Fraggin' Dragon**, p. 48.

Any player characters or major NPCs who were not killed during the yakuza invasion will be tied up and away from the main scene. A single yak soldier is guarding them. Sumiko has identified any magicians among them, removed any fetishes or magical items, and has them gagged and blindfolded. A magician cannot cast a spell if he cannot see. The guard has been ordered to kill the captured magicians at any sign of a spirit appearing.

If Hernandez has accompanied the team back to the hideout, they can kiss all hopes of stealth good-bye. He will go absolutely berserk, charging the yakuza and shooting at Sumiko. Unless the team does something at once, he will be cut down by yakuza swords or bullets.

Now wait a minute, where's Max? Oh, there he is, over by whatever serves as a bar, gulping down a drink. He does not look thrilled, but neither does he look like a prisoner.

The yakuza team's mission is to kidnap Maria. They will do whatever it takes to get her out of there alive. However, they do not want to leave any loose ends that could betray their involvement in her disappearance. If they see Hernandez with the shadowrunners, they will try to kill all the witnesses and take Hernandez's corpse with them for use in their alibi. If they believe that they can deceive the shadowrunners, they will try to give the impression that Hernandez sent them and may leave some survivors to spread that impression.

That's about it. When the fight is over, go to **Boy, I'm Glad That's Over**, p. 46.

DEBUGGING

If the yakuza kill off all the good guys, then Part One of the story ends on a real down note. Even if the shadowrunners trash the yakuza, things can get pretty dark. Naturally, it is the gamemaster's decision on who lives, who dies, and so on.

If the player characters are all captured, pinned down, or what-have-you, the gamemaster can always try to give them one last chance. Have Maria reach for the chip unit, as if she is giving in. Sumiko steps closer. Maria grabs her arm, yanking the mage's pistol out of its holster with her free hand. She puts a slug into the yakuza guarding the prisoners, then a brutal elbow strike from Sumiko doubles her up on the ground. While the yakuza deal with these surprises, it gives the shadowrunners one or two turns to try to escape their bonds, summon a spirit to help them, or other ploys.

BOY, I'M GLAD THAT'S OVER

At this point, Part One of **Maria Mercurial** is over, for better of worse. This section describes the outcomes most likely to occur.

All shadowrunners killed or hospitalized.

This is no fun, but it leaves the gamemaster with many choices about how to proceed. The players may decide to throw in the towel, which means that the bad guys' plan succeeds. Alternatively, the players whose characters bought it can choose new Archetypes or design new characters who have been contacted somehow to save Maria. It could be surviving members of the first team or an hysterical Hernandez who calls them in. Or it might be a Contact—a cop, a rocker, or anyone else who might have an interest in Maria or this case. Pick up Part Two of the adventure with this new team.

Part Two changes drastically in this case. Most of the time-consuming legwork goes out the window and the shadowrunners must race against time to save Maria. Somewhere there will be a clue that points the surviving runners or any new player characters to the Taetzel Building.

We suggest picking up the adventure with **Maid in Japan**, p. 53. Hernandez, one of the surviving shadowrunners from the first team, or even someone from the Underworld can mention the Sorayama signature. This is a slim lead, but will take the team to the Dragon Knights' mainframe and then to the Taetzel Building.

Alternatively, if there are surviving shadowrunners present when Maria is handed over to Perianwyr, they will observe Sumiko's death, as described in **The Fraggin' Dragon**, p. 48. This could lead to a wild chase after the dragon, ending with a battle royal at the Taetzel Building.

Maria will be holding out against giving Morgan what he wants. The neural work Sorayama did is more powerful than anyone could have expected. Just as it let her sublimate the addiction to dreamchips into her musical performances, it has given her some control over access to the sealed memory she carries. She is not consciously aware of this, only that she does not want these people messing with her mind and so she digs in her silver heels and fights them every inch of the way. Within reason, she holds out just as long as it takes the shadowrunners to get to the Taetzel Building. She will be starting to break and deliver Texamachach's report when the team invades the base. See **Into the Lair**, p. 61.

Maria re-addicted to dreamchips.

If Maria jacks in the dreamchip, the aftereffects of the trip will leave her in a coma. She will require immediate hospitalization or her nervous system may burn out. Even if medical intervention saves her life, there is no guarantee that her sanity will survive intact. She spends Part Two of the adventure in a hospital bed, suspended between life and death. Hernandez provides any backing the team needs, assuming his funds were returned.

Maria is still the major objective for Morgan and his Dragon Knights, and must be protected from them.

Maria killed.

The shadowrunners have failed their mission. If they cannot avenge Maria, they lose face. Morgan and the Dragon Knights will still be out to get the shadowrunners, as they represent a dangerously loose end to the plan.

Hernandez killed.

If Hernandez is killed, the bad guys better make sure Maria is either dead or hooked on BTLs. If she is functional, she will bankroll the shadowrunners to track down whoever is responsible and make him pay. Of course, they'll have to strap her down to keep her from going along with them, for Maria will want to take vengeance with her own hands.

Maria and Armando both alive and relatively healthy.

Looks like a happy ending. Not only are they reconciled as performer and manager, but they seem to be on their way to letting their deeper feelings for one another emerge. The shadowrunners should enjoy a moment of basking in this reflected warmth before tying up one last loose end…

What about Max Foley? Good question! At the first sign of trouble, Max dove for cover. Like most lower forms of life, his capacity for survival is enormous. Unless a player character wastes time finding him and knocking him off during the fight with the yakuza, Max will survive.

So, what do we do with Maxie? An amusing scene will take place if the team's decker ripped into his bank account and the shadowrunners now demand payment of the balance owed them. Max will try to punch up the credit and his credstik will keep insisting he is broke.

If the shadowrunners decide to just kill the little slime, he will talk his head off, telling them everything he knows, which is not much. As far as he knows, the Shigeda wanted to get control of Maria's career. The only thing Sumiko ever let slip to him was that larger issues were involved relating to something called New Horizons.

If they let Max go, his dying scream from outside the hideout will signal the beginning of Part Two, in **The Fraggin' Dragon**, p. 48. If Max is already dead, Part Two still gets off to a hot start when a blast of flame sets the hideout on fire!

A gamemaster who is feeling somewhat ornery can let the players relax, even start discussing karma awards, then read them the opening text for **The Fraggin' Dragon**.

THE FRAGGIN' DRAGON

TELL IT TO THEM STRAIGHT

If Max Foley was allowed to leave, read the players this paragraph:

Suddenly, you hear a shrill, agonized scream. If you listen closely, you can hear the words, "Hey, not me, am I riiiIIIIIIIGHEEEEE!" There is a hollow, roaring sound. If you run to the door in the direction of the sounds, you will see a charred corpse, wreathed in flames, flopping on the ground. The melted remains of a quantity of gold jewelry identifies the body as Max Foley's.

If Max is already dead but Sumiko escaped from the battle, read them this instead:

Suddenly, you hear a woman's voice raised, chanting a mage's words of power. The mystic words turn to a shrill scream of agony as a hollow, roaring sound erupts. If you run to the door, in the direction of the sounds, you will see a charred corpse, wreathed in flames. The remains of an ornate walking stick lie nearby, wreathed in eldritch sparks of light as well as smoldering fire. As you look, the sparks dim and die.

If Foley and Sumiko are both already dead, skip the preceding paragraphs and read this one. Read this one whether you read one of the preceding paragraphs or not:

Before you can react, the roof of the hideout bursts into flames. The fire runs through the structure. Time to go, shadowrunners, unless you want to risk burnout this early in your careers.

When the survivors get clear of the building, they will see a local wino staggering about in the glare of the flames, yelling incoherently. If they go close enough to listen, he will turn toward them and blurt out this story:

"I saw it, I tell ya! A fraggin' dragon, man! One minute, there's this car fulla suits, y'know? They're running around wavin' fraggin' swords an' guns an' all an'…an' then…there's this dragon! It rears up and just burns this one dude down like he was, I dunno, like, y'know like nothin', an' then the thing spits fire all *over* The Fraggin' place, and the suits are in their car an' the buildin's on fire an' the wiz-worm's up in the sky and its like *laughin'*, and Ghost, I feel fraggin' awful, arrgh-huck, blaaaw…"

The wino throws up all over a player character and passes out. After sleeping it off, he will not remember any of this.

BEHIND THE SCENES

Kyle Morgan and Perianwyr have decided that Sumiko left too many loose ends. Max Foley has to go. For that matter, so does Sumiko (if she survived the fight). The original plan has collapsed and Morgan wants to clean house before he tries to save the situation.

The Dragon performed the hit, and followed up with a strike against the hideout. If the gamemaster wants an alternative, Sumiko herself could be Perianwyr's target, with Morgan under orders to prevent the capture of anyone who might reveal Aztechnology's role in this affair. Though she may have escaped from the shadowrunners, they know who she is. The mage has become expendable.

Since the Shigeda have failed, Morgan must personally attempt to get the data out of Maria's head. He does not particularly want to succeed at this mission, but if he fails, he may find himself lethally out of favor with Aztechnology.

The hideout will catch fire. If the building is a solid construction like a modern condo, this may be only a minor problem because the place is equipped with firefighting gear. If the hideout is a derelict building, a fire is a much more serious matter. Getting out of a burning building requires everyone to resist 4M3 damage from flames, smoke, and falling debris. The flames may also cook-off heat-sensitive explosives. Anyone loading explosive rounds? Roll 1D6 for each set of explosives, which will go off on a result of 6. Armor helps a little: half the Impact Rating is effective against the heat and debris. If people try to pick up gear, unconscious characters, and so on, each turn they spend in the burning building requires another Body Resistance Test against 4M3 damage.

Franklin Co. firefighters will arrive on the scene within ten minutes, accompanied by a DocWagon, capable of any necessary first aid. More severely wounded characters can be delivered to a hospital. Of course, this will be a "real" hospital, with computers that can be decked, reports that have to be filed with Lone Star, and so on. Not a secure site. If the team wants to get covert medical care, they will have to get to their street doc under their own steam (or maybe bribe the DocWagon crew).

OTHER NPCs

PERIANWYR

If the team gets into combat with Perianwyr, consult the **Cast of Characters** for the Dragon's statistics.

DRAGON KNIGHT AGENTS

This is a typical squad of the agents Morgan has available for the mission. Each agent is a Corporate Security Guard type (**Shadowrun**, p. 165).

These are standard corporate grunts, tough and ruthless. They will surrender if they cannot escape from a fight that has gone sour. Their mission is to secure the Dragon's escape route. If they shoot down the shadowrunners or pin them with rifle fire, they will attempt to withdraw from the fight. If captured, they won't talk easily, resisting even the strongest Interrogation with a Target Number of 10. If the shadowrunners do manage to trick (or beat) information out of them, they only learn that the agents got their instructions from a heavily scarred Indian with a thick, Aztlan accent (Mixacopotec, Morgan's bodyguard). They will *not* admit to any connection with Aztechnology!

If turned over to the police, the agents will vanish within hours, sprung without a trace by the influence of the corporation.

Skills:

Add Heavy Weapons 3 to their skill lists.

Gear:

All are armed with FN HAR Rifles. Ammo 20 (Clip). Damage 5M3. Laser Sight (–1 Target Number to hit) and Gas Vents 2.

All are armed with Fichetti Security 500 pistols. Ammo 10 (Clip). Damage 3M2.

Two agents are also carrying missile launchers, loading Anti-Vehicle Missiles (6D4 against vehicles and 12D8 against personnel). 4 missile loads (4 reloads each)

All wear Partial Heavy Armor with Helmets (Ballistic 7, Impact 5). Smart Goggles. The armor is a black and gray "urban camo" pattern, with no identification.

DEBUGGING

If the surviving team members are unable to get clear of the building, Franklin firefighters can arrive more quickly to rescue them. This is especially important if Maria is trapped inside.

The team may try to find the Dragon. Perianwyr is using an Invisibility Spell, so the only way he can be detected is with radar or magic. Using radar or astral senses, a character may spot him by making an Unresisted Intelligence Test with a Target Number of 3.

If someone assenses the Dragon and follows him in astral space, the dragon will attack astrally. If they dodge away, Perianwyr can land, go astral himself, and deal with the impertinent magician. He will not land, however, until he is safely under air cover from his lair, as described in the next paragraph.

If the team tries to chase Perianwyr in a plane, copter, or ground vehicle, using radar or other means to track the dragon, they are able to pursue him to the fringes of the Barrens. As the beast starts his descent, however, a team of agents on the ground begins to fire missiles at the player team's vehicle. In the confusion, they will lose sight of Perianwyr, though they will now know that he is lairing somewhere in this area. It is a maze, though. Old buildings, a big abandoned factory (yes, the old Perfekto plant), abandoned office blocks, the usual debris. There are some big, new billboards bearing the slogan "New Tomorrows FROM New Horizons" on some building sites, and some blocks are partially demolished. If they decide to investigate New Horizons, go to **Scanning The Horizon**, p. 51.

If the players do not pursue the Dragon, go to the next section, **Where To, Guys?**

TELL IT TO THEM STRAIGHT

Well, here's another crossroads. You guys thought you had this mission sewn up solid, and now you run into some really hot opposition. A Dragon! I mean, an honest-to-Ghost Dragon flies in outta nowhere, fries Max, and almost cooks the rest of you medium well. What the heck is going on here?

Past experience suggests that you start looking for answers quick, because your playmates aren't going to give you much time to figure things out.

BEHIND THE SCENES

This section covers the actions that the shadowrunners might take to track down these new opponents before they tackle Kyle Morgan and his team, followed by full sections describing these possibilities. Indeed, if the adventurers play their cards right, they may be able to blow the plot by digging the Perfekto data out of Maria's head and going public. With nothing to gain by further attacks, the corp team will pull back and head for home, hoping their powerful bosses will be satisfied with their explanation of what went wrong.

POSSIBLE ENCOUNTERS

If the players' team pursues the clue about New Horizons, the details are in **Scanning The Horizon**, p. 51. This section leads them to the Dragon Knights' base of operations in the Taetzel Building. They may also reach this section if they chased Perianwyr back to his lair in the Barrens, because the Taetzel Building is in that area, and it has New Horizons signs all over it.

If the player characters decide to follow up on Maria via the signature on her skin job, 84 Sorayama, go to **Maid in Japan**, p. 53. Some players might have noticed it from the picture on the front cover. If not, the gamemaster makes an Unresisted Intelligence Test for each player against a Target Number 5. Any successes mean that the character remembers getting a glimpse of the name. If Maria is hospitalized, it may also trigger this section, for her physicians will have numerous questions about her cybermods.

If the players are stuck and need some more clues, proceed to **Digging For Dirt**, p. 56. This section contains various pieces of information the shadowrunners can get by asking the right questions or just doing legwork. These clues lead pretty directly to the Dragon Knights and are intended to get the adventure moving.

If the team is still stuck or they refuse to move against Morgan and his Dragon Knights, then the Knights come after them in the section entitled, **Knock, Knock**, p. 57. This will be a strike or strikes by the agents of the Knights. To eliminate the threat, the runners must go in after them. They will get enough clues to locate the Dragon Knights' base in the Taetzel Building (if they survive the attacks, that is).

DOING LEGWORK

Many of the above-mentioned possibilities involve "legwork"—going out and looking for facts by interviewing people, asking questions, or doing research. Any character may make one Legwork Test each day. Skills that allow legwork include Etiquette in some appropriate subculture (street, business, political, and so on), Computer or Decking, and Negotiation or Interrogation. The gamemaster can allow others that seem appropriate. Make an Unresisted Success Test for the skill, using Target Numbers specified in the different subsections.

Keep a running total of the group's successes from Legwork Tests. When the total reaches a given number, give them the clue(s) indicated in the appropriate section.

For example, three characters are doing legwork. One uses Computer Skill, another follows up Contacts using Etiquette (Business), and a third is out asking questions using Etiquette (Street). The first day, they roll 1, 4, and no successes, respectively. Their total for the day is 5 successes. They would have uncovered any facts with a Success Rating of 5 or less in the particular section of the adventure that they are investigating. The next day, they continue their efforts, and roll 1, 1, and 2 successes. Their total is now 9, and they get all clues with a value of 9 or less.

Keep separate totals for each section. If two characters are in **Scanning The Horizon** and another is checking Maria's past in **Maid In Japan**, total up their successes separately. Successes collected in one section do not count for clues in another.

SCANNING THE HORIZON

BEHIND THE SCENES

This section comes into play if the shadowrunners start to investigate New Horizons Development.

As they accumulate successes in Legwork Tests each day, the gamemaster begins to give the team all the clues up to and including their current Success Total.

If the shadowrunners decide to check out the Taetzel Building, it is described in **Into The Lair,** p. 61.

The Target Number is 4.

AVAILABLE INFORMATION

5 Successes   New Horizons began developing properties in the Barrens last month. Work went quickly for a week, then stopped at all sites on the same day, leaving all jobs unfinished. Work stopped about a week before Maria found the incriminating documents on Armando's computer. Coincidence?

8 Successes   The New Horizons computer system is a wide-open, Blue network. (If a decker goes to verify this, it is true). This suggests that the corp keeps its real business off the Matrix, i. e., on a system that cannot be accessed by phone. The Blue system contains perfectly legal zoning and licensing agreements and lots of publicity releases describing how New Horizons is going to revive the Barrens.

12 Successes   New Horizons began to acquire the Barrens properties about a year ago.

14 Successes   The only area of the neighborhood that New Horizons has not bought up is the old plastics plant that used to be the center of the area's economy, and an office block about a kilometer away from it. Both the plant and the office block (the Taetzel Building) belong to a company called Perfekto Polymers.

16 Successes   The neighborhood about two kilometers from the area that New Horizons is developing will also get a major expansion when Mitsuhama opens a new regional manufacturing and sales center there next year. Local property values for housing the thousands of new employees will go into orbit!

18 Successes   Perfekto Polymers is a wholly owned subsidiary of Aztechnology. When the local plant shut down virtually overnight in 2045 and the company pulled out of the area, the neighborhood economy collapsed and the area turned into a slum.

20 Successes   New Horizons is a front for the Shigeda yakuza syndicate. If the shadowrunners obtain this clue, someone has noticed the team's constant probing for information. Select at random one of the characters doing legwork, and have two yakuza soldiers attack him. They will not kill him unless he defends himself with deadly force. Their orders are to beat him severely enough to put him in the hospital with Moderate or Severe wounds as a warning to mind his own business. Fortunately, Sumiko did not get all her information back to the gang, so the Shigeda do not know that this character is one of those who mucked up their plans for Maria Mercurial.

22 Successes   Street people in the area noticed one other burst of activity after New Horizons stopped construction in the area. About a week later, several unmarked vans and several dozen workers spent three days outside the old Taetzel Building, an office block near the center of the slum. Once they left, squads of toughs began to patrol the area for a radius of several blocks around, brutally driving away anyone they encountered.

OTHER NPCS

YAKUZA GOONS

Even yakuza gangs have ordinary, workaday goons. These are two of them. They are legbreakers, not professional, cyber-to-the-max killers like Sumiko's soldiers. They will even run away if they find an opponent is too tough to handle.

They are professional enough not to carry ID, but one of them is missing the little finger of his left hand, a well-known yakuza trademark. Presumably, he hosed up in the past, and his superiors accepted his apology by cutting off his little finger in the traditional ritual. Also, both goons are tatooed with *irezumi*, extensive designs covering the upper arms, shoulders, and back, another hallmark of a yakuza gang member.

Yakuza Goons will try to attack one of the characters doing the legwork. They will follow him, and if they see an opportunity, will close in to work him over, first with their stun batons, then with feet and fists. They will only use their guns if the player character pulls a deadly weapon.

Attributes
Body: 4
Quickness: 4
Strength: 7
Charisma: 2
Intelligence: 3
Willpower: 2
Essence: 3
Reaction: 6*

Skills
Firearms: 4
Stealth: 4
Unarmed Combat: 5
*Reaction increased +2 for Wired Reflexes.

Dice Pools
Defense (Armed): 5
Defense (Unarmed): 5
Dodge: 4

Cyberware
Muscle Replacements: 1
Wired Reflexes: 1

Gear:
Fichetti Security 500. Ammo 10 (Clip). Damage 3M2.
Stun Batons. Damage 5L2 stun. See **Shadowrun**, p. 118, for special effects).
Lined Coats (Ballistic 4, Impact 3).

CONDITION MONITOR			
MENTAL		**PHYSICAL**	
Unconscious.> Possibly dead			< Unconscious. Further damage causes wounds.
Seriously > Wounded.			< Seriously Fatigued.
Moderately > Wounded.			< Moderately Fatigued.
Lightly > Wounded.			< Lightly Fatigued.

CONDITION MONITOR			
MENTAL		**PHYSICAL**	
Unconscious.> Possibly dead			< Unconscious. Further damage causes wounds.
Seriously > Wounded.			< Seriously Fatigued.
Moderately > Wounded.			< Moderately Fatigued.
Lightly > Wounded.			< Lightly Fatigued.

MAID IN JAPAN

TELL IT TO THEM STRAIGHT

You've been wondering about it since you met her. Where did Maria get that incredible cyberware! In the aftermath of the fight with the Yakuza Goons, you finally got a clue. High on one slim, muscled silver thigh, you noticed an imprint. Taking a closer look, you could make out the words "84 Sorayama." But what could that possibly mean?

BEHIND THE SCENES

Sorayama is the handle of a brilliant, eccentric Street Doc in Chiba, the Japanese prefecture outside Tokyo that is the world center of hot cyberware. Chiba cyber is top-of-the-line, leaving anything else buried in the dust, chummer. With the right connections and plenty of nuyen, this is the place to get bodmods no one else can touch.

When Reynaldo Texamachach decided to have his new possession done over to his specifications, he wanted nothing but the best. He handed Sorayama an open-ended credstik, a wish-list, and a young girl. Three months later, Sorayama handed him back Maria, the 84th creation in Sorayama's "Ultra" series.

If any of the characters have Biotech AND Etiquette (Street) Skills of 4 or more, they will recognize the Sorayama name without any Legwork Tests. Otherwise, make a secret Unresisted Biotech Skill Test, Target Number 6, for any team member with Biotech Skill. If the test succeeds, the character remembers hearing about Sorayama.

If Maria is hospitalized, either for wounds or dreamchip-addiction, the attending medico can call the characters' attention to the signature as well. If he's a Street Doc, he may even be able to identify Sorayama.

Whether Maria is hospitalized or not, any medico who works on her will report to the shadowrunners that her neural circuitry shows a mass of sealed memory installed in her silver skull. It is designed to look like normal control circuits for her bodyware, but the technology shows up on some of the new scanners. If no medico ever examines Maria, the only way the team can get this information is by following this lead to Sorayama or else by decking the Dragon Knights' mainframe (see **Decking the Knights**, p. 58).

Given a clue to Sorayama's involvement in Maria's past, it is a safe bet that the shadowrunners will figure he did her cyberwork. If they want to pursue it, they can do some legwork, see if the man has a computer they can deck, or hop a plane to Chiba.

If they do legwork: The appropriate skills are Etiquette (Street) or Biotech, and because Sorayama is so secretive, the Target Number is 8. Remember to total up each player's successes.

SORAYAMA LEADS	
3 successes	Sorayama does about 50 modifications a year, and his prices run from three to five times normal. He is a hot cyberdoc, who treats his skills like an art.
6 successes	Rumor has it that Sorayama does a lot of borderline stuff for corporate clients, modifying people into toys for their pleasure, like human *bonsai* trees.
8 successes	Sorayama only signs work he considers a masterpiece, his "Ultra" line of modifications. Each Ultra is a unique job. 84 Ultra would have been done sometime in 2044
10 successes	A Seattle fixer who specializes in hot cyberware is willing to sell you Sorayama's latest system address for a mere 1,000¥.

If they try to deck Sorayama's clinic: To get to Japan, the decker must move into the local RTG (Green-4, for Seattle) and enter the Chiba prefecture RTG (Orange-3). Having done so, the decker can hunt up Sorayama's clinic through "directory assistance" (**Shadowrun**, p. 100).

The decker will be in for a surprise when he enters the system. Because Sorayama has purchased customized IC architecture for his computer, the Matrix takes on a classy Japanese look. Nodes turn into pagodas, while IC appear as samurai warriors or monsters from ancient Japanese legends.

DEBUGGING

Even if the decker is lousing up the deal and the system is kicking his butt, the gamemaster may want to go easy on the character until he gets to the file on Maria. After that, if he gets greedy and starts trying to scoop out loot, let the IC go wild. That does not mean making the decker fail, however. If he starts to lose, fudge the rolls so that he beats the IC, and then make the file on Maria the next thing he gets. Now, having let him survive when he should have been dumped, throw another piece of IC at him that kicks him out of the system.

SORAYAMA SYSTEM MAP KEY

NODE 1

SAN. Red-3 (No unauthorized visitors wanted!). Trace and Dump 4. The SAN appears as the towering gate house of a classic samurai castle. A high, pagoda-like tower blocks the decker's way, with a massive, closed and barred gate in its center. If the decker fails to deceive the gate, then its attempt to warn the system takes the form of clanging bells and shrill gongs.

NODE 2

SPU. Orange-5. Access 6. The SPU appears as an eight-sided walled enclosure, guarded by a fierce-looking samurai warrior armed with a conch-shell trumpet. If the IC is not deceived, the warrior tries to sound the alarm on his trumpet.

NODE 3

SPU. Green-4. Barrier 3. The SPU appears as an eight-sided garden, with bonsai trees set among lovingly raked stones. In the center, a clear pool shimmers. In its depths, data transfers flash like golden fish. A high wall blocks one end of the garden. This is the Barrier Ice.

NODE 4

This is an I/OP connecting to a sophisticated range of bioscanners, holographic imaging systems, and so on. It allows Sorayama to feed data on his subjects directly into the computer. The I/OP appears as a long gallery running along the castle walls. Each window in the gallery wall presents a different scene. Each scene is the input from an imaging device.

NODE 5

These are Slave Modules controlling a vast array of surgical gear. The SM appears as a busy courtyard filled with craftsmen. Though they are dressed as Japanese peasants of the samurai era, they wield glittering, high-tech surgical tools, and on their workbenches are quivering pieces of human bodies.

NODE 6

SPU. Red-4. Killer 4. This SPU is a large armory, crammed with armor, katana, and other samurai weapons. It is guarded by a mighty warrior in full armor, wielding a great katana.

NODE 7

Datastore. Red-4. Access 5. Tar Pit IC. The node appears as a busy counting house for the castle's business transactions. The entrance is guarded by a "nightingale floor, " a feudal Japanese burglar alarm that makes loud screeching noises when someone walks across it. If the IC is not deceived, that is just what it will do. In addition, when Tar Pit is triggered, the floor drops away, revealing a bottomless pit. The lost utility will fall into the pit, vanishing from sight.

Each file in the store appears as a scroll or, in the case of databases, a rack of scrolls. This is Sorayama's main customer-record store. There is one big database of about 5,000 Mp. Scanning this shows transactions for typical modifications on about a thousand clients. A typical entry might read: "Joe Samurai/Muscle Implant Level 2/150,000¥ for reduced invasive surgery/performed 03/23/49." These data have no particular value.

There is also a smaller database, about 1,000 Mp in size. These are the records for Sorayama's "masterpieces." If using Browse to search the database, the keywords "84 Sorayama," "Aztechnology," and even "Mercurial" may work. Reading the file will also work, as there are only about 120 entries. The decker will find the one containing references to Maria with no trouble if he takes the time to read all 1,000 Mp of data. Maria's file is 20 Mp in size, and can be downloaded without the need to download the whole 1,000 Mp database. Relevant portions of the file read:

"Ultra design #84 commissioned 06/13/44 by Johnson-*san*, whom my sources identify as an Aztechnology rep. Subject Maria Aguilar, apparently under standard indenture to corporation. Almost reluctant to undertake modification, but even when nature accidentally creates such beauty, art can improve on it. Estimate time to completion at 90–120 days.

"Specifications include novel dermal replacement (see attachment), heightened reflex response, improvements in musculature, and various cortical implants. Additional fee specified for the new ultra-secure sealed memory space, modified to be transparent to most current scanning technology. Direct interface modifications also route primary datalink plugs through pleasure/pain centers of brain. I have pointed out to the client that this will intensify many cybernetic activities to the point of endangering subject's sanity. Simsense, direct data access, even synthlinking a simple music generator will have profound effects on the subject. This is acceptable to the client."

The entry continues for several hundred pages, with accompanying medical data, pictures of Maria in various stages of modification, and so forth. Notes indicate that the use of a synthlink to train her in the use of her neural circuits had the greatest success. Sorayama notes: "Subject appears to find the concentration involved in synthlinking sufficient to control possible psychological trauma due to the pleasure/pain interface of the datajack."

Near the end, the following appears: "Per instructions from client, applied customized simsense chip at illegally high amplitude to subject until dependence was established. Subject response indicated profound addiction after ten days of two exposures per day."

At the end of the medical report, a brief note is appended: "Surprised and not a little pleased to observe this subject recently on tri-vid. Apparently, she was released from indenture and is now artiste of renown, under name Maria Mercurial. Though the music is not to my taste, the performance of her modifications is obviously still at appropriate standards. Perusing references to her in various popular journals, I suspect that the subject suffered psychological damage from extended exposure to high-amplitude simsense addiction, but has somehow overcome the dependency. Judging from the intensity of the synthlink performance, this may be ascribed to the effects of the pleasure/pain interface of the datajack, so that music became, in itself, an influence stronger than the simsense addiction. This may be the subject of an interesting future monograph."

Finally, there is an entry dated about two months ago. It notes that an Aztechnology rep requested a copy of the file, which was delivered to a system address in Seattle, on LTG #6206. This is the system address for Kyle Morgan's mainframe in the Taetzel Building (see **Decking the Knights**, p. 58.)

NODE 8

Datastore. Red-4. Black IC 5. This is Sorayama's Research and Development data area. This Datastore appears as a quiet courtyard in a Buddhist temple. It is spare, clean, and bare of any vegetation. The courtyard surface is raked gravel, with eight rocks positioned artfully here and there. Each rock is covered with artwork, which is actually a file. One might be a *sumi-e* ink painting, another might look like an intricately carved *netsuke* piece, while a third is a gracefully painted fan. If the gamemaster is not comfortable inventing such images, the best bet is to represent each file by an ink painting.

New designs for cybermods, circuit designs, and other valuable tech are here. There are eight files, worth 20,000¥ per 10 Mp, with sizes of, respectively, 50, 80, 120, 50, 40, 60, 90, and 40 Mp. If selling the data through a fence (see **Shadowrun**, p. 147), this stuff counts as high-tech and hot loot! Sorayama will be looking for the thieves through yakuza connections. If they discover the meet, half a dozen yakuza will show up to kill the thieves and their fence. (Yakuza code in this case calls for death to both vendors AND receivers of stolen goods.) Use the yakuza Soldier statistics from **Yakkity Yak**, p. 42.

Gamemaster's Option: As an alternative to selling this stuff, the team finds that each file contains designs for cyber-modifications (gamemaster's choice) to be installed for 25 to 50 percent less Essence loss than usual, though at double the price. These are custom specifications, which the data-thieves cannot mass-market. That is, the shadowrunners cannot go into business selling these mods for 20¥ a pop in some chop shop.

NODE 9

The CPU. Red-5. Trace and Burn 6. System operation permits transfer of funds (500,000¥) which must be fenced normally. For purposes of downloading, this is a 100 Mp file. The credit file is guarded by Black-4 IC.

The CPU appears as the Great Hall of a mighty *daimyo*, or samurai lord. He sits brooding upon a dais at its far end. Beside him is a huge lacquer chest, open to reveal the glint of gold. Behind the chest looms the figure of an *oni*, a Japanese demon, bearing a powerful longbow (the Black IC). The doors to the room are guarded by two Fu dogs, the fierce lion-hounds that guard Japanese temples from evil. Flames and smoke issue from their gaping mouths. These represent the Trace and Burn Ice. If the two dogs are released, one will remain to face the decker in combat while the other runs into the distance, howling and snuffling, to trace the decker's path. If the decker deceives or kills either of them, the IC crashes.

If the system goes into External Alert, Sorayama has access to the services of two deckers from a Japanese yakuza syndicate. These are "Major League" opposition (**Shadowrun,** p. 116), and Sorayama can contact them in ten turns if his system displays an External Alert. In deference to Sorayama's wishes, these deckers maintain samurai Persona while in his system.

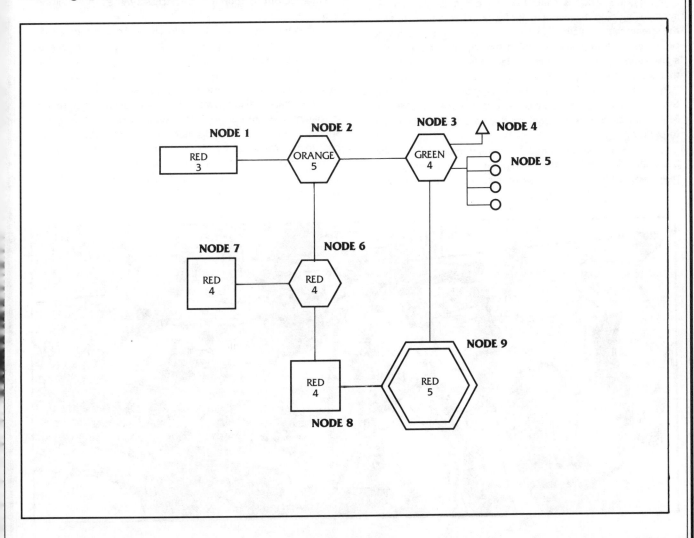

DIGGING FOR DIRT

BEHIND THE SCENES

There are several loose ends the shadowrunners can decide to tie up. Some of them contain clues about what is going on here.

If they ask Hernandez about Maria's therapy to kick dreamchips:

Hernandez will be able to get you in touch with Ms. Kenner, Maria's therapist. If he vouches for you, she will tell you the following:

Maria's modifications included an interface that ran her datajack through the limbic region, the pleasure/pain center of the brain. Using the jack provides stimulus to the brain centers. Maria has tremendous control over the signals involved in synthlinking, and this was a major factor in her therapy to kick the dreamchip addiction. In most cases, using the datajack produces random pleasure or pain stimuli, depending on the signals she is passing through the jack. Ms. Kenner points out that only scum-sucking drek would inflict this kind of modification on someone. However, the surgery is so complex that trying to undo it could produce serious damage. In addition, Maria refuses to consider anything that would affect her ability to perform.

Maria's responses during the therapy indicated that she had been addicted to a custom chip, one tuned to her specific psychological and neurological profile. That is an expensive process, not something a poor prostitute working in a Barrens dive could afford. When Hernandez found her, Maria was jacking large quantities of "average" street chips to try to assuage her need for the custom stuff.

Ms. Kenner is still Maria's therapist. God knows the poor woman needs one! She will *not* discuss her patient's current status unless convinced that it is in her interest to do so. If the shadowrunners can pull that off, either by roleplaying or skill use, then she gives them the material that is in Maria's "Personality Profile", in the **Cast of Characters** section, p. 70.

If the shadowrunners have the dreamchip from Down to the Wire **analyzed:**

An Unresisted Biotech Success Test can be used to analyze it, but a microtronic tool kit is also necessary. The Target Number is 5.

The chip is so powerful it could kill most deckheads. Unlike most BTLs, it is a very high quality chip. Most BTLs are burned into cheap silicon imported from Ghost-only-knows-where. This looks like a studio-quality simsense chip. The chip was made in Aztlan and the model is about five years old.

The analysis also shows that this is a custom chip. That is, its parameters are designed to give a maximum trip to one specific individual. If the chip analysis is done by a Biotech who has treated Maria, or by Ms. Kenner, her therapist, or if the results of the analysis are discussed with such a person, he or she can compare the chip parameters to their records on Maria and verify that it is tuned to her profile.

KNOCK, KNOCK

TELL IT TO THEM STRAIGHT

Man, you've been out plugging away at this drek forever, or at least it feels that way. Time to stretch out and get some slee…Hey, did you hear something?

Your security systems yell warnings as you check the window. Suits—maybe half-a-dozen of them—armed for bear. Looks like the opposition just got tired of waiting. Who's that streety-looking dude with them? Oh, wiz, it's Snout, that little Ork snitch. If you get outta this in one piece, you're gonna have words with the little creep.

BEHIND THE SCENES

Even if the characters are not doing legwork or finding clues, they know too much. Morgan has sent in some muscle to silence them. Permanently. If the characters have been digging up evidence, then he is even more nervous.

His own contacts have been busy keeping track of the shadowrunners' activities. Snout, a small-time goon, has fingered one of the runners for Morgan, leading a group of agents to the character's home or hideout.

The attackers are the same kind of standard agents we met back in **The Fraggin' Dragon**, p. 48. They outnumber the player characters by 50 percent (round up fractions of a guard), depending on how many players are present. Thus, if the guards are tackling only one player character, there are two guards. If

there are four player characters in the scene, there are six guards, and so on. The corp goons are armed as in **The Fraggin' Dragon**, but are not carrying missile launchers. If the runners try to flee in vehicles, the goons will pursue in a modified Chrysler-Nissan Patrol 1, armed with a medium MG and twin missile launchers loading AVM missiles.

Their orders are to kill the shadowrunners. They are coming in hard and fast, and are not worried about stealth. If the runners have any kind of security, it will warn them of the attack, but they only have five turns to get ready for it. Surprise is impossible, because the corp killers are ready for combat. Any booby traps that are set up can be used, however. The goons will try to break and run for it if they are ever outnumbered by two-to-one. That is, the team must kill or incapacitate two-thirds of the original strike force.

Resolve the fight. If the runners are all killed, so much for that. End of story. Any survivors can easily locate Snout, buying a round of drinks for the house at his favorite bar, The Down And Out. If the shadowrunners display ready weapons, no one in the place is going to argue if they have a little discussion with Snout.

If they threaten him even a little, he will reveal that he was tapped by a scarred-up Indian from Aztlan. The guy paid him 500¥ to scope out the runners' hideout. Two goons blindfolded him and led him to the meet, but he sneaked a peek and knows the location. It was in the Taetzel Building.

The shadowrunners can follow this lead to **Into the Lair**, p. 61.

DECKING THE KNIGHTS

BEHIND THE SCENES

Several paths can lead the team into the Dragon Knights' mainframe. This system is interconnected with the Taetzel Building's own computer system. In fact, a decker who jacks in to scope out the building system may even find himself ghosting into the Knights' computer.

A decker can slash into the system, grab what he can, and run. Heck, if the shadowrunners get the unlock code from Node 3B, they can pull the information out of Maria's head and go public with it. If that happens, the Dragon Knights will be out of town within three hours, and there will be an unexplained fire at the Taetzel Building that removes all evidence of their stay.

Alternatively, the decker may try to hit the system and suppress the building's security systems while the rest of the team hits the site physically. The possibilities of this scenario are dealt with in **Into the Lair,** p. 61.

In the event that an external alert is triggered, Lin Hwang will jack in to deal with it. There are numerous possibilities if the system is decked, because it holds the data that define the entire situation, and in 2050, data are power.

TAETZEL BUILDING/DRAGON KNIGHTS COMPUTER MAP KEY

This is two systems in one. The Taetzel Building's normal control mainframe is System A. The Knights' own mainframe is System B. Nodes are marked as A or B on the Map and in the Key. An Alert on one system will not trigger Alert status on the other, and shutting down one system leaves the other unaffected. System operations are also local to the system in which the decker is located, i. e., the CPU in the Taetzel Building system cannot give orders to the Knights' system and vice versa. The one exception is the Security Terminal on the Knights' system (Node 8B), which *can* interact fully with the Slave Modules controlling building services and systems (Node 3A). Special software running on an interface module (Node 7B) makes this possible.

NODE 1A

SAN. Green-4 Access 5. This is the "public" access port to the Taetzel Building system, used for ordering supplies, handling deliveries, alarms to fire or police, and so on. Security is a bit higher than on many SANs, but not remarkably so for an office space. Of course, it is rather remarkable to find a working SAN for an abandoned building.

NODE 2A

SPU. Orange-3. Barrier 5.

NODE 3A

Slave Modules. Orange-7. These control all building systems: air conditioning, elevators, and power to all floors EXCEPT the 28th floor. The Dragon Knights have independent power feeds to this, their headquarters area, bypassing the computer controls. The modules also allow access to security cameras and the anti-intruder devices that the Knights have attached to them. A decker in this node can activate or deactivate any camera or device as a system operation, but if the Security Terminal (Node 4B) is manned, his action may be observed. Note the extra successes needed for his Computer Skill Test. Roll 1D6. If the die roll exceeds the number of successes rolled, then the Security Terminal shows that something has interfered with the system and may trigger an External Alert.

Do not reveal the exact rules governing detection to the decker, but if he thinks to ask whether operations in this module might be detected elsewhere, tell him yes. If the player is this careful, the gamemaster can also tell him he has noticed control logics leading into the Matrix. He can see them running along the datapath out the "bottom" of the module. They imply the existence of a console somewhere else in the system, monitoring this Slave Module.

If the decker scans through the Slave Modules, he will find that they control the cameras throughout the building. These will let him observe the monsters guarding the place and the number of guards present.

If Maria has been captured, he will see her tightly bound, but not visibly damaged, in the gymnasium on the 28th floor (see **Into the Lair,** p. 61). She is apparently unconscious. A visibly upset dwarf armed with a heavy pistol is standing guard.

The decker will also be able to observe a phone conversation through the camera in Kyle Morgan's apartment. Morgan is talking to his Mr. Johnson, who is using a sophisticated scrambler that distorts his voice and features. The dialogue goes something like this:

JOHNSON: I've never heard of a case where anyone could withhold information in sealed memory after the recovery code had been given. Have you any theory as to how the woman is doing it, Kyle?

MORGAN: Gods, you people had that Japanese butcher rewire the girl's nervous system like a Christmas tree. How do I know what Sorayama's circuits are doing? All I know is that she is fighting us with everything she has and...

JOHNSON: That will do. Our time is extremely short. You will bring additional pressure to bear to break her resistance. Any means necessary, do you understand?

MORGAN: Sir, she is at the edge now. Any more stress could kill...

JOHNSON: Any means necessary, Mr. Morgan. Do I make myself clear?

MORGAN: Of course, sir. As always.

JOHNSON: I shall expect your report within the hour, Kyle. Upper management is watching this case very closely. Any further delay could undermine your excellent record.

Mr. Johnson breaks the connection. Morgan stares at the screen for a moment, then turns away. He has been juggling something in his hand during the conversation. He looks down at it, then drops it on the carpet and stalks out of the room. If the decker zooms the camera in on the item, he will see that it is a CD of Maria's first album, "Night Tears. "

NODE 4A

The CPU. Orange-4 running Trace and Report 6. Normal enough for an innocent, commercial mainframe. Of course, in this case, a successful Trace means that a load of corporate killers will be on the way within minutes. (Send two squads, i. e., six guards, using the Agent statistics from **The Fraggin' Dragon,** p. 48, or **Into the Lair,** p. 61).

NODE 5A

A Blue-4 Data Store that contains operating records for the Taetzel Building. All files are unprotected. The main database is 150 Mp. It shows that the building closed down in 2045. There are periodic maintenance entries until a month and a half ago, after which records indicate systems being brought back on line, checks on power, water, and so on.

Most of the refitting activity was on the ground floor and the 28th floor. The building map shows that the 28th floor formerly housed the executive office suites.

Supply requisitions since then are in quantities sufficient to support perhaps two to three dozen people. In addition, a number of special orders for meat—not nutrisoy, but real, honest-to-Ghost meat, like from cows—are recorded. Hundreds of kilos of it. There are also records of enough beer to drown a few dozen men.

NODE 6A

SAN. Green-4 running Killer 5. Leads into System B, the Dragon Knights' mainframe.

NODE 1B

SAN connecting to satellite feed dish on roof (see **Into The Lair,** p. 61). Red-4 running Trace and Burn 3.

NODE 2B

SPU. Orange-4 running Blaster 6.

NODE 3B

Data Store. Green-5 running Access 6. This is Kyle Morgan's private data area. It contains :

•A summary of the mission, including the history of the Perfekto Plastics plant, the story of Texamachach's death, the problems with New Horizons, and the fact that Maria is carrying the waste-tank location in her sealed memory.

•A resources list that names the Dragon Knights cadre. Holopix attached.

Kyle Morgan, Team Leader (handsome dude, isn't he?)

Perianwyr, Team Second and Occult Services (holy steaming drek, that's a picture of a DRAGON!)

Jorge Mixacopotec, Security (a scarred man with Indian features)

Blackstone, Technical Services (a Dwarf)

Lin Hwang, Computer Services (a middle-aged Oriental)

•A message file: "Maximum security rating: Unlock code is Silver Virgin. Do *not* reveal to anyone with security clearance under Level Beta. Use with extreme discretion. Do not trigger unlock in presence of individuals not cleared for Class 1 material."

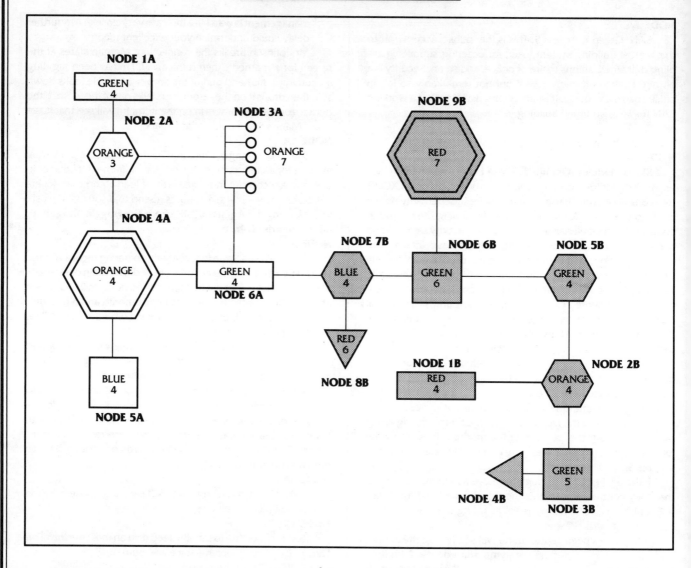

·A message file: "The Dwarf's family attempted an unauthorized exit from the corporate dependents' facility. The woman was apprehended but the child is missing and presumed to be in the hands of dissident elements. The woman succumbed to intensive interview techniques. As a result, Blackstone's continued loyalty to the corporation is open to question. Accordingly, you are instructed to liquidate this agent upon completion of the mission."

·The mission "cash box. " The file contains controls for an open credit account with Orbital Credit Bearnaise. It is locked with Scramble 8. Unlocking the file allows a credit transfer of up to 750,000¥, subject to usual laundering requirements. No download required. This file is a program that will automatically transfer the credit into a secret account, from which it can be fenced.

NODE 4B

The Command Terminal. From here, the user can override the Security Terminal, operating any Slave Module function in Node 3A. He can order a system shutdown of *either* mainframe. He can also order any CPU system operation. The decker can do these things with a successful system operation test.

NODE 5B

SPU. Green-4 running Barrier 5.

NODE 6B

Data Store. Green-6, no IC. The Dragon Knights' operating records. Personnel files on 15 corporate agents. Four files are annotated to show that these agents have been trained as "handlers. " Inventory of the armory (see **Into the Lair,** p. 61). Various requisitions for vehicles, fuel, and so forth.

NODE 7B

SPU. Blue-4. A system operation here can crash the special security interface that ties Node 8B into Node 3A. If that happens, it is immediately obvious to the Security Terminal operator, but the crash cuts his controls to the building security until both mainframes can be shut down and restarted.

NODE 8B

The Security Terminal. Red-6. The user can perform any of the system operations allowed on Node 3A. In addition, if the decker performs system operations here, they are *not* detected by the terminal operator. From here, he can make things look normal to the terminal operator.

NODE 9B

The CPU. Red-7 running Black IC 5. Nasty.

TELL IT TO THEM STRAIGHT

The Taetzel Building...Almost 30 years old, this was once a mid-size office block that is now a 28-story derelict in the middle of a slum. Built in the Festung style popular in the late 2020s, it has solid, concrete walls up 20 stories or so, with mirrored armor-glass windows on the top floors where the bosses hung out.

You've scoped it out, mapped its forbidding exterior. Now it's time to take it.

BEHIND THE SCENES

This is it. The shadowrunners have to hit Morgan, the Dragon Knights, and their goons here or the bad guys will keep on picking at them until they go under.

Following are several maps of the Taetzel Building. The first is the basic plan, showing every floor. The second shows the building's exterior, including the roof. It would be easy enough to scope out the building's roof from taller structures, even from a kilometer or so away. However, the area *under* the helipad where Perianwyr lairs is not visible from that distance. Let the players see a copy of the second map.

The only two floors that are actively manned are the ground floor and the 28th floor. All the other floors are empty, perhaps holding some dusty office furniture, but with minimal lighting, and so on.

If the Dragon Knights have captured Maria, they are holding her in the gymnasium on the 28th floor. Morgan is about to apply a combination of BTL chips and drugs to break her resistance when the attack begins. Because he is so reluctant to apply this kind of torture, an interesting alternative to the final showdown is described in **The Long Fall**, p. 65.

All the Dragon Knights are present in the building: Morgan, Blackstone, Mixacopotec, and Lin Hwang. Their initial positions are noted on the building map keys. Perianwyr is in his lair on the roof.

Besides these forces, Perianwyr has provided his friend with some typically draconian resources. Besides men and machines, Morgan's base is guarded by two griffins, a cockatrice, and a basilisk!

Each of these creatures was trained by Perianwyr. Each has only *one* handler among the agents. If that handler is killed or incapacitated, the creature goes wild and attacks the nearest target, whether a shadowrunner or a bad guy. The creature will continue to hunt ferociously, stalking through the building seeking prey. Only Perianwyr or Kyle Morgan can take control of a creature whose handler has been killed. Note that Perianwyr can control the cockatrice or basilisk from Astral Space, as these creatures are always actively present on the astral plane. The griffins, however, are not. This is convenient for the Dragon, who cannot fit inside the building physically unless he starts knocking over walls.

DEBUGGING

The shadowrunners will have the advantage of surprise until they lose it. Morgan does not really expect them to attempt to take his base. Unless their decker is blocking the security cameras, as soon as they walk into an area monitored by the cameras, the bad guys will know they are there. Any guard can try to trigger an alarm, but the decker can block that, too. All the guards carry portable phones, which cannot be blocked by the computer. Therefore, the gamemaster must use his judgement. The shadowrunners have to take out the guards before they can make a call for help on the phone.

Once surprise has been lost, the guards' actions will depend on whether the Knights can track the shadowrunners on the security cameras. If they can, they will maneuver their agents in two equal groups, trying to surround them. Mixacopotec leads one of these groups.

If they cannot track the runners, they will divide the remaining agents into four equal groups. One will be stationed on the 28th floor. A second is placed on the ground floor. The other two start to search the building, working down from the 28th floor. One group descends via the central stairs, the other via the back stairs. The elevators will be disabled, either through the computer or by killing the power to the elevator on the roof. All groups of agents will be in constant communication via portable phones. Mixacopotec will be leading the group down the central stairs.

If the runners break the agents, the remaining Knights on the 28th floor will get weapons from the armory and try to shoot their way out. Note that Blackstone will NOT fight. Moreover, he will actively use the building security system to help the shadowrunners if they reveal the fate of his family to him. Kyle Morgan will join Perianwyr on the roof.

Whether the shadowrunners corner Morgan on the roof or on the 28th floor, their showdown with the chief of their enemies is dealt with separately in **The Long Fall**, p. 65. If Maria is a prisoner and they enter the gymnasium either by chance or to rescue her, then go to this same section to deal with that situation.

TAETZEL BUILDING MAP KEY

BASIC PLAN

The exterior walls of the Taetzel Building up to the 20th floor are Reinforced Concrete (Barrier Rating 32). On floors 21 and up, they are Reinforced Armor Glass (Barrier Rating 8). The top eight floors were "executive country," and a view was considered a "perk," even during the troubled twenties.

The building has a core containing a bank of four passenger elevators flanked by stairwells and lavatory facilities. At the back of the building are a freight elevator and additional stairwell.

Interior walls and doors are Normal Construction Plastic (Barrier Rating 4).

Security cameras are present on all floors. In addition, servoguns have been installed at specific locations on the ground floor and 28th floor. The statistics for these automated shotguns are:

Firearms "Skill" 6. The aiming mechanism only works at Short or Medium range.
Damage: 4M3
Initiative: 20 (no roll required)
Armor: Ballistic 3, Impact 0. The weapons are partially concealed by their housing, and thus attacks against them are at +2 for Partial Cover.
Body: 4

A decker can take over servoguns if he is in one of the appropriate nodes in the Taetzel Building computer.

EXTERIOR GROUNDS

The grounds are surrounded by a three-meter-high, chain-link fence. The fence is guarded by pressure sensors that will alert the security center on the 28th floor if anyone tries to climb or cut the fence. These sensors can be spotted by making an Unopposed Intelligence or Electronics Test with a Target Number 4. They can be disarmed by making an Unopposed Electronics Test with a Target Number 6.

Two agents patrol the perimeter, taking 15 minutes to complete a circuit of the grounds.

The Main Gate (A)
The gate is locked, but can be opened from the Security or Command Terminals on the 28th floor.
Parking Lots (B)
Empty, with weeds growing out of cracks in the asphalt.
Rear gate and loading dock entrance (C).

THE ROOF

Helipad (1)
The helipad is raised about five meters from the roof. Underneath is a cozy little den. The lair contains:
- the bones of several sides of beef, gnawed very clean.
- a 100-liter vat, which proves to contain beer, if anyone checks.
- an expensive trid unit, with a voice-activated control unit. The contents of the music library consist of thousands of rock and roll recordings, catalogued chronologically, ranging from music of the early 1950s to the latest Maria Mercurial hit.

Perianwyr will be here unless Kyle Morgan is under attack on the 28th floor. If the bad guys lose the battle indoors, Morgan and Peri will be up here, waiting for their final face-off with the shadowrunners.
Air-Conditioning Plant (2)
Communications Shack (3)
The satellite-link dish is the feed into the SAN to the Knights' mainframe.
Elevator Core (4)
The elevator machinery is in the housing on top of this structure.

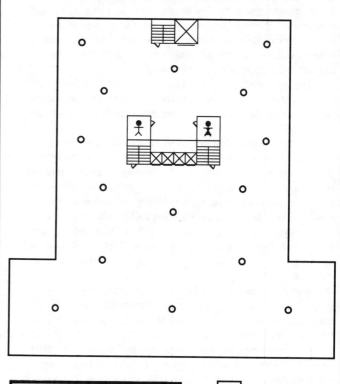

The Taetzel Building

Basic Floor Plan

☐ = 5 Meters

○ = Load Bearing Pillar

GROUND FLOOR

Lobby (1)

The lobby is visible to the agent sitting in guard booth (Area 2). It is equipped with a security camera that also has a servogun attached. The gun is an automatic weapon that can fire from the guard booth or the Security Terminal at any location in the room. It does 4M3 damage.

Guard Booth (2)

From here, the one guard present can view the lobby (Area 1) through armorglass panel. The guard can trigger the servogun covering the lobby. A firing port lets him shoot his FN HAR into the lobby. He can also trigger an alarm throughout the building unless his alarm control is overridden on the building computer.

Basilisk Lair (3)

This is an office converted to a lair for the basilisk, which is present in the room with its handler. It can easily hear any weapons fire in Areas 1 or 2 and will move to cover Area 4.

Inner Lobby (4)

This lobby leads to the elevators, and is guarded by a security camera and two servoguns.

Loading Dock (5)

The cockatrice and its handler guard this area, which is also equipped with a security camera and a servogun. There are two Chrysler-Nissan Patrol-1s parked here, modified as described in **Knock, Knock**, p. 57. Stacked against the east wall are several packing cases, marked "Office Supplies. " They contain a pair of missile launchers and 8 AVMs.

Rear Entrance (6)

Two agents guard this entrance. The corridor is also covered by a security camera and a servogun.

Elevator Core (7)

Unless the action is blocked on the computer, the car will freeze at the 11th floor if the shadowrunners take the elevator. After three turns, the cables will cut loose, the brakes will not engage, and everyone inside must resist 4D2 damage when the car plows into the bottom of the elevator shaft.

To get out of the elevator, the shadowrunners must blow or force the doors open, or smash loose the access hatch in the ceiling. The elevator doors are normal construction plastic (Barrier Rating 4). Forcing the doors open requires an Unresisted Strength Test with a Target Number 8 (6 if using an appropriate tool). One success opens the doors enough to let one person at a time move through. Three or more successes force the doors wide open, with enough space to let any number of people pass through them in the course of a turn.

Smashing open the ceiling hatch requires an Unresisted Strength Test with a Target Number 4. However, to clamber through the hatch requires an Unresisted Quickness Test with a Target Number 5. If the test fails, the person who blew the hatch is stuck in it until his next action. Someone can push or pull the character through the hatch by making an Unresisted Strength Test with a Target Number 4, but this costs him his action. Anyone who gets through the hatch can grab a handhold and hang on safely when the elevator car goes. They can then easily clamber out the 11th-floor elevator door.

Note that if a decker is controlling the building systems, he can pull this same stunt on any bad guys who take the elevator. The agents will use the elevator to move around the building, unless they suspect that their system has been invaded. Once they stop trusting the system, they will take the stairs.

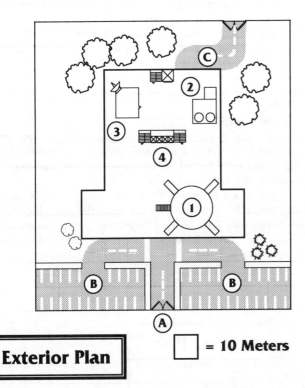

Exterior Plan   ☐ = 10 Meters

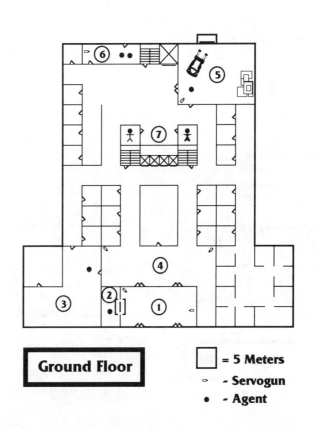

Ground Floor   ☐ = 5 Meters

◦ - Servogun

• - Agent

28TH FLOOR

Elevator Core (1)

Covered by two security camera/automatic servogun combinations and two agents.

Kyle Morgan's Quarters (2)

This area boasts luxurious furnishings and several photos of stunning women seated with Morgan in his sports car. ("Cripes, isn't that Beauty Shannon, the simsense star?") There is also an old flat photo of a gangly, teenaged Morgan leaning against the side of a Dragon. If the player characters remove this from its frame, they will find the words "Llawrgwynedd 2022" written on the back in faded ink.

A cyberterminal is on a desk in one corner of the room. This is the Command Terminal (Node 4B). Each attempt to crack security on the terminal and gain access to the system takes ten minutes base time. To get in requires an Unresisted Computer Skill Test, with a Target Number 8. Divide the base time by the successes. Minimum is one minute. The terminal displays a menu of available options.

Morgan is here during the fighting, monitoring things from the Command Terminal. If his access to the system is locked out, he will move to the security center (Area #14). If his forces are losing the battle, he will move up onto the roof.

Mixacopotec's Quarters (3)

This area is furnished in a spartan fashion. A heavy wooden club, set with obsidian spikes, hangs on the wall. Mixacopotec will not be here, as he is leading a squad of agents into the thick of the fight.

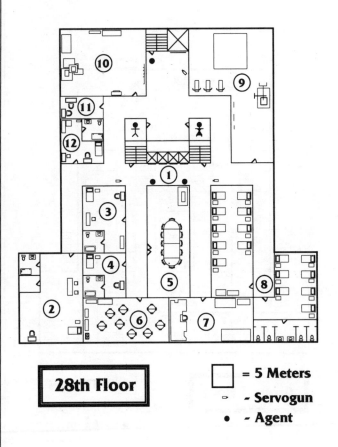

28th Floor

☐ = 5 Meters

⌐ - Servogun

• - Agent

Lin Hwang's Quarters (4)

These quarters display a typical modern decor, with a cyberdeck on a table next to a cyberterminal. Lin is here, monitoring system performance, and of course, jacked in if he detects a system invasion.

Conference Room (5)

This room contains a large oak table with room to seat twelve. A very expensive trid unit, with large projection tank, dominates the center of the table. If the contents of its memory are displayed, there are photos of Maria and Hernandez, maps of their homes and offices, and charts showing the progress of Morgan's plans to date (mostly with various paths terminating in dead ends). There may be photos of at least some of the shadowrunners.

Kitchen and Dining Area (6)

This area is well-stocked with food and equipment such as oven, microwave, and refrigerator. There is a securely locked, very sturdy cabinet. Smashing it open will reveal an array of liquor bottles.

Computer Room (7)

The Knights' mainframe is installed here.

Barracks Area (8)

This area has been converted to hold bunks and footlockers, military-style, with space for 16 persons.

Gymnasium (9)

Several exercise machines, racks of weights, and a wrestling mat are in the center of the room. If Maria was captured, she is here. See **The Long Fall**, p. 65, for ideas on how this might be worked into the final showdown.

Armory (10)

The Armory has a heavily reinforced door. To open its maglock requires a valid maglock cardkey (each of the Knights has one) or a maglock passkey and an Unresisted Electronics Skill Test, with a Target Number 8.

The armory contains a rack of six FN HAR assault rifles and four Ares Predators. Stacked nearby are several cases of various kinds of ammo. Two missile launchers and several boxes of various missile types are stored against one wall. A locked case contains grenades, explosives, and various timers, fuzes, and detonators.

Security Center (11)

The Security Terminal is installed here. The center is manned by Blackstone and an agent, and Morgan may be here if the Command Terminal has been locked out or compromised.

Blackstone's Quarters (12)

The area is a typical technomancer's litter of components, equipment, tools, and so on. One corner has been cleared out as a living area. On a table by the bed is a holo of Blackstone, a pleasantly smiling Dwarf woman, and a small Dwarf child, maybe two years old.

THE LONG FALL

BEHIND THE SCENES

If Maria is NOT in the Dragon Knights' hands when the shadowrunners corner Kyle Morgan, he will simply attack them all out, blazing away with a pistol. He will not seek cover, he will not parlay, he will not surrender. Caught in a dilemma between duty to his job and admiration for Maria, he chooses this way out. He is not fighting to kill so much as he is fighting to die.

If Morgan is indoors when the gunfire erupts, the window behind him shatters inward under the furious strength of a Dragon. Perianwyr can be seen hovering outside. "Kyle, get down. Get DOWN, blast you!" Morgan pays no attention. Peri will be unable to loose his flame at the shadowrunners without incinerating Morgan as well.

On the roof, Perianwyr will fight the runners with either spell or fire.

If they score a wound on him, Morgan's iron concentration will break. He will stare at the wounded Dragon momentarily, then pull a grenade from under his armor. It is recommended that the gamemaster let the next shot from a shadowrunner "kill" Morgan before he can arm and throw the explosive.

When Morgan is blasted out of the window, Perianwyr will erupt with a deafening bellow, loose a blast of flame at the runners, and dive out of sight, roaring his grief. Still flaming, he dives after the falling body, and both disappear into the clouds of smoke that his flames leave in the air.

That is the last the player characters will see of them. Morgan is certainly dead, for no one could have survived that! But then again, the body is never found. The Dragon simply vanishes.

If Maria IS a prisoner, then the final scene takes place in the gymnasium, where she is being held. The runners break in to see the following tableau: Mixacopotec is standing over Maria's bound figure, holding a syringe and dreamchip injector. Half-conscious, she is hissing insults at him in Spanish and Aztec. He is grinning horribly. Even if the shadowrunners killed Mixacopotec during the fight for the building, he is here again, like a character from some slasher movie, ready once more to do nasty things.

Morgan is standing with his back to the window, a faint smile on his face. He knows that the fight is over and it is time to die. Pulling his gun, he orders Mixacopotec to back away from Maria. The Aztlan merc pulls his own weapon. Two shots ring out at once. Slowly, Mixacopotec topples over, dead.

Morgan murmurs softly, "And then there was one." Without another word, he turns and attacks the shadowrunners, with the same conclusion as above.

OTHER NPCS

KYLE MORGAN

Kyle Morgan is in his mid-40s and still as fit as a man half his age. He is one of the Sixth World's premier assassins. What, you've never heard of him? See how good he is. He is known, under various aliases, as a rally driver, a useless drone on the glitter scene of the international "jet set" of 2050.

For the last ten years, he has worked for Aztechnology. He is the corp's court of last resort, to be sent in when matters get desperate.

In 2022, Morgan befriended Perianwyr, the newly awakened Dragon, and they have been partners ever since. Though their current employment is profitable, they have big plans for the future, and are becoming increasingly disenchanted with the goals of their corporate masters. Their own plans for the future will make them powers in the Sixth World, or get them killed trying. Morgan and Perianwyr share an empathic link that makes each experience the other's emotions.

Morgan is especially unhappy with the present mission. Knowing Maria's history, his sympathy is all on the side of his victim. For this reason, he stands largely aloof from the combat. If it goes against him, he withdraws to face the end with his closest friend.

Attributes
- Body: 5
- Quickness: 6
- Strength: 5
- Charisma: 5
- Intelligence: 4
- Willpower: 4
- Essence: 2.3
- Reaction: 9*

* Wired Reflexes increase Reaction.

Dice Pools
- Defense (Armed): 1
- Defense (Unarmed): 5
- Dodge: 6

Cyberware
- Datajack
- Smartgun Link
- Wired Reflexes: 2

Gear
- Armor Jacket (Ballistic 5, Impact 3).
- Ares Predator (smartgun). Explosive Ammo - 10 (Clip). Damage 4M4. −2 to Target Number to hit.
- Ares Viper Slivergun. Ammo 30 (Clip). Damage 2M3 (flechette ammo).
- Ranger Arms SM-3. Ammo 6 (Magazine). Damage 6S2.

Skills:
- Firearms: 4
- Languages
  - French: 4
  - Spanish: 5
  - Welsh: 6
- Leadership: 7
- Negotiation: 6
- Pistol: 8
- Racing: 7
- Rifle: 7
- Unarmed Combat: 5

CONDITION MONITOR

	MENTAL	PHYSICAL	
Unconscious.> Possibly dead			< Unconscious. Further damage causes wounds.
Seriously > Wounded.			< Seriously Fatigued.
Moderately > Wounded.			< Moderately Fatigued.
Lightly > Wounded.			< Lightly Fatigued.

PERIANWYR

In 2022, Perianwyr awoke from his centuries-long sleep, deep in a Welsh cavern. He emerged, ravenous after his hibernation and found himself among a flock of sheep. In draconian fashion, he devastated the flock, glutting his hunger. Still shaky after his sleep, and slowed by his crammed belly, the Dragon would have been killed by an irate mob of heavily armed farmers if a local boy had not stood off the mob with nothing but a rusty old shotgun and charisma. That boy was Kyle Morgan.

The Dragon and the young human became friends. They have worked together for over 25 years, gaining wealth and skill in the world's shadows.

Perianwyr regards Morgan as his only friend, the only being for whom he feels affection. He may respect or fear the more powerful members of his own species, but only this fierce and loving human has a fire of spirit to match the Dragon's own. The Dragon is empathically linked to Morgan, feeling his emotions as if they were his own.

Peri disapproves of the current mission for the same reasons as Morgan. He, too, he stays aloof from the final battle, unless Morgan is threatened, which will infuriate him.

Attributes
Body: 15/4
Quickness: 6 x 3
Strength: 40
Charisma: 4
Intelligence: 5
Willpower: 8
Essence: 8
Magic: 8
Reaction: 5

Attack Code
10D3, +2 Reach

Dice Pools
Dodge: 6
Magic Pool: 6

Powers
Animal Control (Reptiles)
Enhanced Senses (Low-Light Vision, Wide-Band Hearing)
Flame Projection (Damage 8L1)
Flight
Low Light Eyes
Wide-Band Hearing

Spells
Combat
Mana Bolt: 6
Sleep: 8
Detection
Mind Probe: 6
Health
Heal Deadly Wounds: 8
Illusion
Invisibility: 6
Manipulation
Magic Fingers: 6

Skills
Languages:
Ancient Celtic: 6
Latin: 5
Welsh: 4
Sorcery: 6

Special Skill
History of Rock and Roll: 6

CONDITION MONITOR

	MENTAL	PHYSICAL	
Unconscious.> Possibly dead			< Unconscious. Further damage causes wounds.
Seriously > Wounded.			< Seriously Fatigued.
Moderately > Wounded.			< Moderately Fatigued.
Lightly > Wounded.			< Lightly Fatigued.

JORGE MIXACOPOTEC

Mixacopotec has fought all his life to get where he is. First, he fought to survive in the stinking slums where he was born. Then he fought as a gladiator in the blood sports of 2050. After a spectacularly bloody career on the trid, he became a mercenary for Aztechnology.

Mixacopotec is a killing machine, heading up security for the Dragon Knights cadre. He only knows two ways to end a fight—by killing his opponent or being killed. So far, he has not been the one to die.

Attributes

Body: 6
Quickness: 5*
Strength: 7*
Charisma: 2
Intelligence: 3
Willpower: 3
Essence: 3.3
Reaction: 6**

Skills

Interrogation: 6
Leadership: 4
Pistol: 5
Rifle: 7
Stealth: 5
Throwing: 4
Unarmed Combat: 8

*Muscle Replacement increases Strength and Quickness.
**Wired Reflexes increase Reaction.

Dice Pools

Defense (Armed): 3
Defense (Unarmd): 8

Cyberware

Cybereyes (Flare Compensation; Thermographics)
Muscle Replacement: 1
Smartgun Link
Wired Reflexes: 1

Gear

Ingram Valiant with deluxe gyro mount recoil compensation (Rating 6). Ammo (Belt). Damage 5S3.
Browning Max-Power with smartgun adaptation. Ammo 8 (Clip). Damage 4M2. −2 Target Number to hit.
Aerodynamic defensive grenades (3). Damage 6M3.
Partial Heavy Armor with Helmet (Ballistic 7, Impact 5).

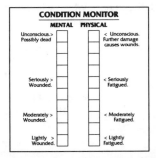

CONDITION MONITOR

MENTAL / PHYSICAL

Unconscious.> Possibly dead — < Unconscious. Further damage causes wounds.
Seriously > Wounded. — < Seriously Fatigued.
Moderately > Wounded. — < Moderately Fatigued.
Lightly > Wounded. — < Lightly Fatigued.

BLACKSTONE

Use the Dwarven Technician Archetype (**Shadowrun**, p. 166).

Blackstone has the stereotypical Dwarven brilliance with technology. He was indentured to Aztechnology by a state creche and was trained, married, became a father, all under corporate regulation. His wife and young son were kept at a "corporate dependents facility." A prison, velvet-lined perhaps, but still a prison. With the families of its less "loyal" employees under control, the corporation feels confident using these employees for sensitive missions.

Blackstone does not much like the missions he is assigned, though he usually enjoys the technical challenges involved. If his family had not been under corporate control, he would have turned against his employers in a minute. Now, his wife freed by death and his son lost in the shadows of Aztlan, Blackstone has no further reason to obey the corp. He will not willingly face death, however, for he still wishes to find his child somewhere in the slums of Aztlan.

CONDITION MONITOR

MENTAL / PHYSICAL

Unconscious.> Possibly dead — < Unconscious. Further damage causes wounds.
Seriously > Wounded. — < Seriously Fatigued.
Moderately > Wounded. — < Moderately Fatigued.
Lightly > Wounded. — < Lightly Fatigued.

LIN HWANG

Lin Hwang was trained as a decker by a Macao gang, a Triad of the old school. He betrayed his fellow members to the police during a major datasteal, kept the take for himself, and wisely fled to the Americas. Should his former associates learn his whereabouts, his life will not be worth a wiped credstick.

He serves Aztechnology for protection and profit. As the price of failure could be exposure to his old Triad's wrath, he can be trusted to fulfill his missions to the letter.

Lin Hwang uses a "Shaolin kung-fu" image for his Persona in the Matrix. The Persona has a sleek, gold-skinned robotic body, and wears crackling, electric-blue tunic and pants. Yin/yang symbols swirl across the fabric. The Persona has glowing neon tattoos on his forearms: a Dragon on the left (which springs to life and breathes fire when he uses Attack in cybercombat) and a Tiger on the right (which roars and absorbs attacks when he uses his Shield utility). When the Persona moves or speaks, a faint tinkling of wind chimes and tiny gongs is heard.

Attributes

Body: 2
Quickness: 4
Strength: 3
Charisma: 2
Intelligence: 4
Willpower: 4
Essence: 4.8
Reaction: 4 (10 in the Matrix)

Skills

Decking: 6
Firearms: 3
Unarmed Combat: 4

Dice Pools

Defense (Armed): 1
Defense (Unarmed): 4
Dodge: 4
Hacking: 6

Cyberware

Datajack, 100 Mp Internal Memory

Gear:

Fairlight Excalibur Cyberdeck with Response Increase 3 (**Shadowrun**, p. 105).

Programs

Bod: 6
Evasion: 3
Masking: 5
Sensors: 5
Attack: 7
Medic: 6
Mirrors: 4
Shield: 4

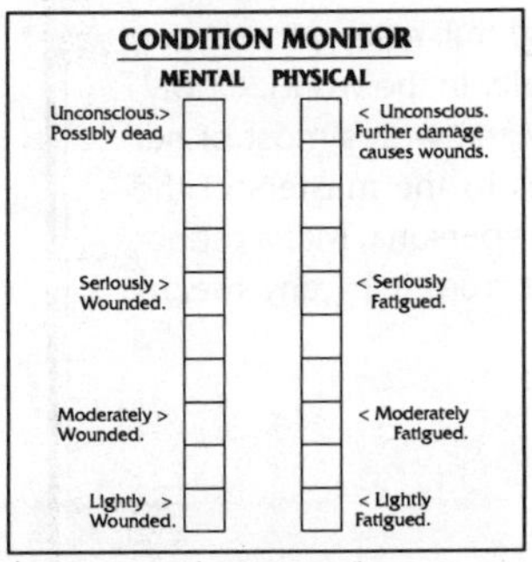

CONDITION MONITOR	
MENTAL	PHYSICAL
Unconscious.> Possibly dead	< Unconscious. Further damage causes wounds.
Seriously > Wounded.	< Seriously Fatigued.
Moderately > Wounded.	< Moderately Fatigued.
Lightly > Wounded.	< Lightly Fatigued.

DRAGON KNIGHTS AGENTS

This is a typical squad of the agents Morgan has available for the mission. Each agent is a Corporate Security Guard Archetype (**Shadowrun**, p. 165).

These are standard corporate grunts, tough and ruthless. They will surrender if they cannot escape from a fight that has gone sour. They obey orders efficiently but are not too swift at taking the initiative.

Skills

Add Heavy Weapons 3 to their skill lists.

Gear:

All armed with FN HAR assault rifles. Ammo 20 (Clip). Damage 5M3. Integral Laser Sight (–1 Target Number to hit) and Gas Recoil Vents (Rating 2).

All armed with Fichetti Security 500 pistols. Ammo 10 (Clip). Damage 3M2.

Two agents also carry missile launchers, loading Anti-Vehicle Missiles (6D4 against vehicles and 12D8 against personnel). Four missiles each (4 Reloads each).

All wear Partial Heavy Armor with Helmets (Ballistic 7, Impact 5). Low-light Goggles. The armor is black and gray "urban camo" pattern, with no identification or rank markings.

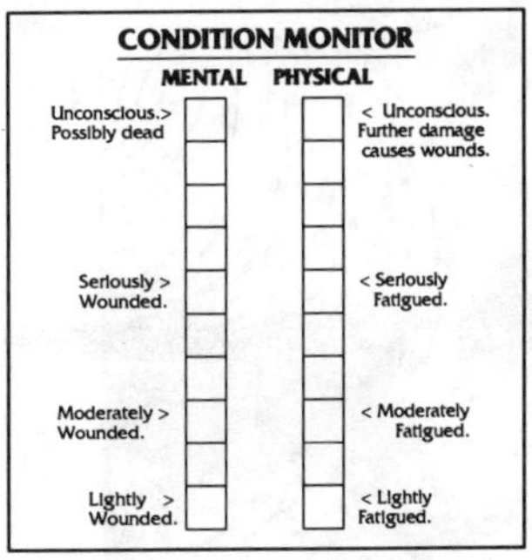

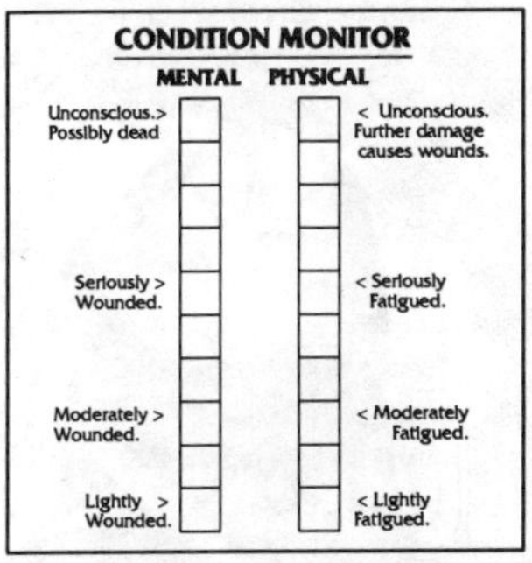

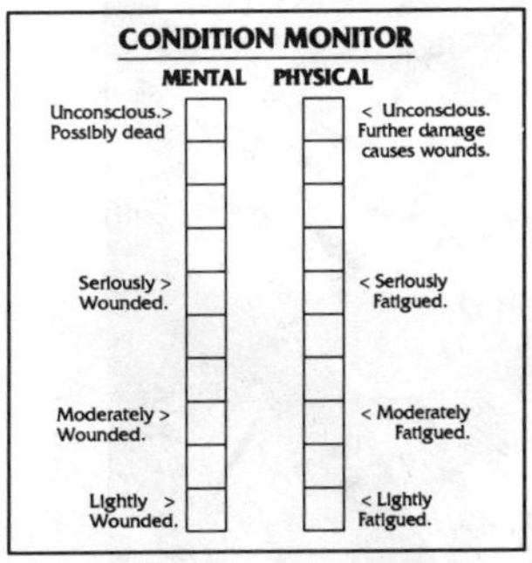

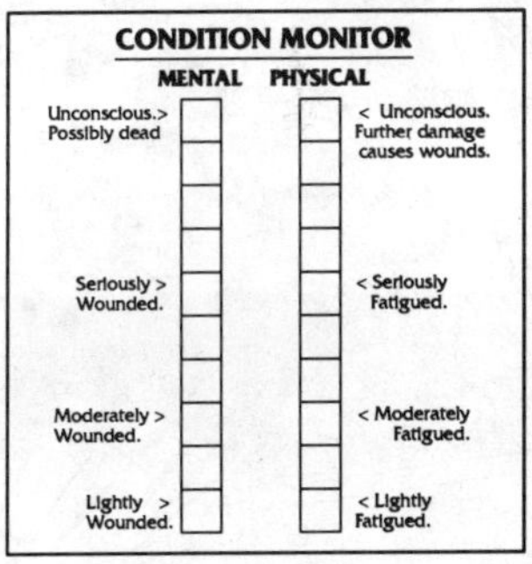

CONDITION MONITOR	
MENTAL	PHYSICAL
Unconscious.> Possibly dead	< Unconscious. Further damage causes wounds.
Seriously > Wounded.	< Seriously Fatigued.
Moderately > Wounded.	< Moderately Fatigued.
Lightly > Wounded.	< Lightly Fatigued.

CONDITION MONITOR	
MENTAL	PHYSICAL
Unconscious.> Possibly dead	< Unconscious. Further damage causes wounds.
Seriously > Wounded.	< Seriously Fatigued.
Moderately > Wounded.	< Moderately Fatigued.
Lightly > Wounded.	< Lightly Fatigued.

CONDITION MONITOR	
MENTAL	PHYSICAL
Unconscious.> Possibly dead	< Unconscious. Further damage causes wounds.
Seriously > Wounded.	< Seriously Fatigued.
Moderately > Wounded.	< Moderately Fatigued.
Lightly > Wounded.	< Lightly Fatigued.

CONDITION MONITOR	
MENTAL	PHYSICAL
Unconscious.> Possibly dead	< Unconscious. Further damage causes wounds.
Seriously > Wounded.	< Seriously Fatigued.
Moderately > Wounded.	< Moderately Fatigued.
Lightly > Wounded.	< Lightly Fatigued.

CAST OF CHARACTERS

Maria Mercurial, Max Foley, and Armando Hernandez are the three main NPCs that the player characters will encounter in this adventure. Descriptions and statistics for these three are included here. Stats and brief descriptions of other NPCs usually appear in the section of the Adventure where the character first comes on the scene.

MARIA MERCURIAL

Maria is in her mid-20s. Indentured at an early age to Aztechnology, her notable beauty attracted the lecherous eye of Reynaldo Texamachach, a senior exec. He had her modified by Chiba cyber-artist Sorayama, and installed her as his companion to fulfill the offices of bodyguard, secretary, and mistress. The story of Maria's final rebellion against his domination is told in the **Plot Synopsis.**

Texamachach addicted Maria to custom dreamchips in order to control her. When she killed him and fled, she also cut herself off from the source of the chips. To blunt the withdrawal from the chips, she turned to regular BTLs, abuse that seriously affected her brain cells. By the time Maria entered therapy with Dr. Kenner, she was suffering from severe personality disorders. Though therapy helped her to kick the BTL habit, she has permanently lost almost all memory of her life before therapy, and is subject to profound personality changes.

She is not, however, a case of classic "split personality." Maria is always in control of her actions, and when her personality changes, she retains all memory of her actions under the previous personality. She has three personas: Amazon, Schoolmistress, and Innocent.

AMAZON

When Maria is Amazon, she is filled with energy, almost to the point of being in a rage. She is abrupt, with no patience for lengthy discussion, and has a hair-trigger temper. The Amazon is her usual personality when performing. Maria often gets wound up very tight in this persona, which makes her seek to unwind through the kind of violent, dangerous encounter described in the **Prologue.** When she feels threatened during such violent episodes, the Amazon takes over as a survival mechanism. The aftermath of such a confrontation usually brings on the Schoolmistress.

SCHOOLMISTRESS

When Maria is Schoolmistress, she is quiet and withdrawn, her emotions repressed. This is a thoughtful, reserved woman, filled with pain at the injustice and cruelty in the world. Oddly, perhaps, it is as Schoolmistress that Maria writes most of her lyrics, even such rage-filled challenges to the masters of the Sixth World as 'Take It To Mister." In this persona, Maria cannot cope with violence, and seeks escape from it by any means possible, even emotional collapse.

INNOCENT

Maria's third and last personality is Innocent. In this mode, she is, in a sense, a child again, in the time before her life was wrenched out of shape to satisfy Texamachach's fantasies. Innocent is friendly, open to people, and trusting. She does not act childishly, but has the naïveté of a child. This personality surfaces when Maria feels safe, a rare occurrence in her life these days. It is the foundation on which Dr. Kenner hopes to build an integrated personality for her patient.

The gamemaster needs to keep these characteristics in mind whenever he portrays Maria, deciding which personality is in control, based on the situation. She can, however, change from one to the other in a flash. In times of tremendous stress, such as **Down To The Wire**, p. 45, she may whip from one persona to another, trying to find a way to cope. If this horrible dilemma is prolonged, she will collapse under the terrible psychological strain.

Some things are constant for all three personas:
- Maria loves and respects Armando Hernandez. She expresses this with warm friendship, but if she trusted herself more, would admit that it is an even deeper emotion. She is torn and confused by his apparent evil and by her own latent feelings. This permits the gamemaster to make her very stubborn about seeing the truth of the bad guy's frame-up.
- Denial is a strong defense mechanism for Maria. She has had to confront things that would drive most people into complete insanity. She will, therefore, simply refuse to deal with threats if they can be avoided. Even the bravest person cannot face continual pain, day after day, without suffering trauma.

Attributes
- Body: 4 (6)*
- Quickness: 5 (6)**
- Strength 4 (5)**
- Charisma: 6
- Intelligence: 4
- Willpower :5
- Essence: 1.3
- Reaction: 5 (7)***

Skills
- Athletics: 8
- Firearms: 6
- Stealth: 5
- Unarmed Combat: 5

Special Skill
- Synthlink Music: 8

*Body increased by Dermal Armor
**Strength and Quickness increased by Muscle Replacement
***Reaction increased by Wired Reflexes

Dice Pools
- Defense (Armed): 1
- Defense (Unarmed): 5
- Dodge: 6

Cyberware
- Cyberears with High and Low Frequency range
- Datajack (with limbic system rerouting)
- Dermal Armor (mirroring effect on limbs and head): 2
- Muscle Replacement: 1
- Wired Reflexes: 1

Gear
- Browning Max-Power. Ammo 8 (Clip). Damage 4M2.

CONDITION MONITOR

	MENTAL	PHYSICAL	
Unconscious.> Possibly dead			< Unconscious. Further damage causes wounds.
Seriously > Wounded.			< Seriously Fatigued.
Moderately > Wounded.			< Moderately Fatigued.
Lightly > Wounded.			< Lightly Fatigued.

MAX FOLEY

Max Foley is in his 50s, short, fat, and balding, with a complexion like week-old nutrisoy. He wears the latest fashions more suited to someone in his teens. He smokes large cigars and wears lots of gold jewelry. Though the gold is real, on Max it looks cheap. Then again, anything that gets within three meters of Max Foley seems to become cheapened. He is, however, a power in the music biz. Like some greasy idiot savant, Max Foley can scope a hundred nowhere bands and pick the one that is going to be a chartbuster.

Max is a talker. If words were food, no one would ever starve around Max Foley. If Part One of the adventure shows signs of flagging, just get Max talking. That will probably send the player characters out to do something in the desperate attempt to simply make him *shut up!*

Max's constant refrain is, "Am I right?" No matter what the subject, Max Foley has been there and done it and knows the score, am I right? This is all total drek, of course, but Foley never lets ignorance shut his big, fat yap, no sir, am I right?

Max is deep in hock to the Shigeda, a yakuza gang, and taking orders from Sumiko Hotoda, who works for the yakuza. Anything he learns about the shadowrunners' plans is phoned in to Sumiko at the first opportunity, to protect his "investment" in Maria's career. Hey, nothing personal. This is business, am I right?

Attributes
  Body: 2
  Quickness: 3
  Strength: 2
  Charisma: 5
  Intelligence: 4
  Willpower: 5
  Essence: 6
  Reaction: 4

Skills:
  Etiquette (Show Biz): 5
  Etiquette (Street): 4
  Firearms: 3
  Negotiation: 7

Special Skill
  Music Promotion: 6

Dice Pools
  Defense (Armed): 1
  Defense (Unarmed): 1
  Dodge: 3

Gear
  Streetline Special. Ammo 6 (Clip). Damage 3L1. Nobody better mess with Max Foley, no sir, am I right?

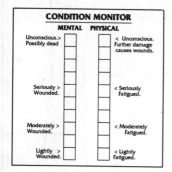

CONDITION MONITOR

	MENTAL	PHYSICAL	
Unconscious.> Possibly dead			< Unconscious. Further damage causes wounds.
Seriously > Wounded.			< Seriously Fatigued.
Moderately > Wounded.			< Moderately Fatigued.
Lightly > Wounded.			< Lightly Fatigued.

ARMANDO HERNANDEZ

Armando Hernandez immigrated to Seattle in the 2020s, at the time of the founding of Aztlan. His liberal political views made him less than popular with the new regime, and he found the freewheeling life of the Northwest more appealing. He is in his mid-40s, a husky man of middle height, with black hair shot through with strands of gray. He is pleasantly ugly, with a nose that has been broken more than once.

Hernandez fell in love with Maria Mercurial the night he first heard her sing. Basically a decent sort, he has sublimated that emotion, all the while promoting her career and helping her learn to make her music, music he believes to be important in an often difficult world. He is deeply hurt by her apparent betrayal of him, but will not oppose Maria's wishes.

When Hernandez learns that he has been manipulated and tricked, he becomes furious, exploding in classically Hispanic oaths and gestures of rage. When he learns that Maria is in danger, however, this theatrical *machismo* vanishes instantly as he turns quietly and grimly to pulling out his weapons and armor from their locker. He intends to join the shadowrunners in attempting to save his silver queen, and nothing will stop him.

Attributes
> Body: 3
> Quickness: 3
> Strength: 5
> Charisma: 4
> Intelligence: 4
> Willpower: 3
> Essence: 6
> Reaction: 4

Skills
> Computer: 2
> Etiquette (Show Biz):6
> Etiquette (Street): 2
> Firearms :4
> Unarmed Combat: 2

Special Skill
> Music Promotion: 6

Dice Pools
> Defense (Armed): 1
> Defense (Unarmed): 2
> Dodge: 3

Gear
> Beretta Model 101T. Ammo 10 (Clip). Damage 3M2.
> Defiance T 250 shotgun. Ammo 5 (magazine). Damage 3M3.
> Lined coat (Ballistic 4, Impact 2)

CONDITION MONITOR

	MENTAL	PHYSICAL	
Unconscious.> Possibly dead	☐	☐	< Unconscious. Further damage causes wounds.
	☐	☐	
	☐	☐	
Seriously > Wounded.	☐	☐	< Seriously Fatigued.
	☐	☐	
	☐	☐	
Moderately > Wounded.	☐	☐	< Moderately Fatigued.
	☐	☐	
Lightly > Wounded.	☐	☐	< Lightly Fatigued.

PICKING UP THE PIECES

For better or worse, the adventure is over now. This section ties up the loose ends.

WINGS IN THE MORNING:
An Epilogue

I felt like death, which was hardly surprising. There are advantages to having a spell-slinging dragon among your associates, especially when you dance in the shadows for a living.

It's a magnificent view of Seattle from the topmost tier of the Aztechnology pyramid. I watched the dawn spread her rosy fingers across the sky and wondered how a blind man could have sung so aptly of that same sight, three thousand years ago. The hills stood stark and black against the mist-filled sky. Sunlight painted the clouds with faint traces of rose and gold.

"What would you say that was?" said a rumbling basso profundo from behind me. "Hope being reborn from darkness?"

"Or is it just giving one last flare before the clouds consume it forever?" I responded.

"You Welsh can be so damn gloomy."

"We've had a lot of practice." Ignoring my friend's answering snort, I limped away from the helipad to the doorway leading into the building. My masters were going to be less than pleased unless I could convince them that this was only a minor loss in their great game. No doubt the clever lads who'd fought to save their silver queen were plenty pleased with themselves right now, though. Well, perhaps they'd earned the right. There'll always be the next time, lads, so savor victory while you may. What the hell, if I'm still alive tonight, maybe I'll go hear Maria sing. Sometimes losing has its compensations.

I had a sudden urge for a smoke. Visions of the blindfold and the final cigarette danced morbidly through my head. My cigarette case had somehow survived intact, but the lighter was gone, God only knew where. I sighed.

"Would you mind?"

"My pleasure, " came the reply.

As I walked in through the door, a sleepy-looking security guard did a double-take, surprised to see anyone wandering about on the roof at this hour of the morning. He certainly hadn't heard a copter land, now had he? Seeing my face, his eyes widened. He wisely withheld comment on the state of my clothes.

"Mr. Morgan, sir! I didn't know you were up here. Let me … Oh, may I give you a light, sir?"

I couldn't help smiling as I took a drag on the black and gold Sobranie. "No thanks. I already have one. " While the guard rang for the elevator, I glanced out the window to savor the sight of sunlight dancing gold on Perlanwyr's widespread wings.

Just another morning in the Sixth World.

AWARDING KARMA

Now that the adventure's over, it is time to award Karma. There are many possible outcomes to the story but in the best of all possible worlds, Maria and Hernandez are exploring their new relationship, the shadowrunners have scooped up oodles of loot, Perfekto Polymers management is slated for wholesale replacement by Aztechnology and the Shigeda, and Kyle Morgan is putting on a new face so he can go to a Mercurial concert without getting shot. If, on the other hand, everyone in sight is dead, Aztechnology has strung up Kyle by his thumbs, and half of Seattle is buried under toxic waste, well, nobody said this was going to be easy.

Team Karma for the adventure is fairly hefty. All surviving team members get 1 point for being alive.

Adventure objectives to fulfill (each worth 1 point of karma):

- Keep Maria alive
- Keep Hernandez alive
- Keep Maria from jacking in the dreamchip
- Find and reveal the data in Maria's sealed memory

The threat in this adventure is truly hairy! Award 3 points to the survivors. Thus, the possible team karma award is 8 points.

ALL THE NEWS

While shadowrunners keep a low profile for themselves, the things they do, or do not do, can leave traces in the straight world. Here are some news items that *might* appear after the run, depending on how things turn out. The gamemaster can hand the appropriate item(s) out to the players, depending on the adventure outcome.

WHO WEEPS FOR THE CHILDREN?

CODA
But tears run down to the ocean,
in rivers that can carve through stone
And in the dawning morning,
we see that we were not alone.

The ones who wept for the future
As they fought to hold back the night
Paid a ransom with their heart's sorrow
And brought back the children for
a golden tomorrow.

—*Closing verse from "Who Weeps For The Children?" copyright 2048, Mercurial Music*

Rapping With A Rocker
by Johnny Disk

—The following is an excerpt from an interview that first
appeared in *Rocker Stars*, the leading rock newsnet, February 12,
2050.

Two years ago, a new sun burst into view in the rocker sky.
People everywhere heard a voice that defied description sing the
opening verse of "Who Weeps for the Children?" Maria Mecurial
had come to town. She's the biggest thing in rock and roll since ME-
109 made the scene in 2046. Some predict her influence will be as
great as that of Concrete Dreams. Angry and awesome, plaintive and
head-pounding by turns, her albums, "Night Tears" and "Puta", have
both sold millions of copies.

I met Maria in her condo here in Seattle. Like many other
novastars such as the Dreams and Red Barron of ME-109, Maria
calls our town her home.

ROCKER STARS: Maria, thanks for having me here.

MARIA: It is my great pleasure, Johnny.

RS: Maria, you came out of nowhere, with this incredible sound and
these songs that say so much, only two years ago. Since then, you've
been a mystery to your fans. What can you tell us about yourself?

MARIA: The only important things anyone needs to know about me
are in the music, Johnny. Where I've been isn't worth drek. Where I'm
going is all that you, or anybody, needs to know or has the fraggin'
right to ask. Do you hear what I 'm telling you, chummer?

RS: Yow, Maria, lighten up. Null perspiration. If you want the past
dead and gone, you got it.

MARIA: I want it buried in a nameless grave.

RS: Right…O. K., so where were we? A lot of your music kicks butt
and takes names. Even ballads like"Who Weeps for the Children"or
"Shadow Storm'"put it to the corps, and songs like "Take It To
Mister" damn near call for revolution. Anything you want to say
about that?

MARIA: Fragging-zed right I do. Too many years, the corps have been
sticking it to you, to me, to "the little people. " Before them, it was
the government goons, or the lord of the fragging manor, or any
oversized piece of slime that had the muscle to get folks thinking he
was the boss. "Take It To Mister" tells Mister Corp, or Mister Boss,
or Mister "I'm-from-the-government-I'm-here-to-help", or any of
the Misters who've ground people down that we aren't going to take
this drek anymore. When I wrote "Who Weeps?", I just thought it
was sad. When I wrote "Take It To Mister", I wanted the slotting
bastards in power to pay for their crimes.

RS: Has there been any pressure on you because of this message in
your songs?

MARIA: Yes, sometimes extreme pressure is brought to bear. On the
concert tour last year, several of my appearances were picketed by
protesters from organizations that are nothing but corporate front
groups. However, can any person of conscience let such things stop
her? I accept this as part of the price I pay to make the music I must
make. It is, perhaps, a sign that I am achieving a small victory over
these persons—to make them fear me and my music even to a small
degree.

RS: You've been called a woman with many different voices. It is as
if you change sometimes from song to song. Just talking to you now,
even…

MARIA: I do not wish to discuss this. Each of my songs is different,
and sometimes one must become the music, whether it is sad or
angry, violent or calm. As to my personal life, I have already told
you…

RS: No offense meant. You're one of the few performers to consis-
tently work solo these days. Everything in the performance is slaved
to you through the 'link. No backup, no other controllers.

MARIA: I find that synthlinking my own performances, without the
need to accommodate an ensemble performance, is more to my taste.
I can express my music in my own way. It is doubtless a vanity. Yet
if I make the sound sing, it is my own victory, and if I fail, I cannot
blame it on others.

RS: You sat in on Cartwright's acoustic jam last year at the Penumbra,
but your concert work is always synthed.

MARIA: Yes, the guitar is, oh, like my own toy. I don't know if I could
share it. It's too personal, in my concerts I mean. Warren is so sweet.
He'd heard me playing at home one evening, where some of us were
just kicking back after a gig, and went, well, just *wild* about how he
liked it. I was *really* embarrassed that Warren Cartwright liked my
playing. He can make you cry, or dance, or anything when he plays,
and he liked *me*. So when he called to say he wanted to do the set—
no synthing, no amps, just acoustics and old-fashioned miking and
everything—and when he told me who all was sitting in, I thought,
O. K., this is family, this is friends, and did it.

RS: But you won't play acoustic in your own gigs?

MARIA: I couldn't. I'd be too scared.

RS: I don't think anything could ever really scare you.

MARIA: No, that's sweet, but too many things do.

That was all the lady had to say. She turned aside everything I
asked after to small talk. It seems pretty clear to me and probably to
a lot of others that here we have a lady with a past. During the
interview, she shifted several times from one personality to another
in the space of a sentence. We've seen it before. When Zango Wilkes
of Astral Lightning suicided onstage a few years back, he'd been
showing the same pattern. It's the classic sign of a ROM-burner, a
dreamchipper. Maria Mercurial has been a star for two years, and
since she's still alive, I can only hope that means she is off the BTLs.
'Cause boys and girls, this woman is for real, and this reporter hopes
to hear her voice for many years to come.

[*Rocker Stars* will be making an exclusive tridcast of Maria's gig at
Underworld 93 next week. Dial channel 93 on your trid at 2000 PST,
Sunday, February 13. 20¥ service fee. A vid of this interview is
available for download on ROCKNET - Punch in MARIARAP
Only 5¥!]

TAKE IT TO MISTER
by Maria Mercurial

Once, long ago, when troubles came your way
You couldn't take them on yourself,
But you knew just what to do,
To find someone who would help.
When they burn out the farm,
Or ravish your sister,
You put your hat in your hand
And take it to Mister,
Take it to Mister

Then, as they will, all these things changed their way.
The ones who guarded you proved false.
The lord, the patron, the grand seigneur,
Helped themselves and no one else.
So they ravished the land
And whored with your sister,
They made you rip out your pride
And take it to Mister.

Now, we have learned there is another way.
To face the future for ourselves,
We all know what we must do.
If you want to take back what they stole
Feed the rage in your heart
Till it's ready to blister.
Now put your gun in your hand
And TAKE IT TO MISTER!

—"Take It To Mister," by Maria Mercurial,
Copyright 2048, Mercurial Music

If the bad guys' plan works and they have murdered Maria and Armando, give the players News Item 1.

So much for the doom and gloom. If the adventure ends happily with Maria and Hernandez alive and the plot of the bad guys foiled, give the following news items to the players.

Promoter Ices Singer, Self

The body of rocker novastar Maria Mercurial was found today, shot to death. It appears that her former manager, Armando Hernandez, riddled Maria with fire from an automatic weapon before turning the gun on himself.

Reports from a reliable source in Lone Star Security hint that the rock star was found with a killer-BTL chip, a "dreamgate," jacked in. This would confirm the longtime databuzz in the rocker community that the silver-skinned singer had a history of dreamchip abuse. One source also hinted that Hernandez may have been trafficking in BTL, based on records reconstructed from his office computer system.

Maria recently terminated her longtime connection with Hernandez to sign with noted talent agent Max Foley. When reached for comment, Mr. Foley said, "This is a tragedy for the music world. The loss of Maria and my able colleague, Mr. Hernandez, is a sad moment for all of us, am I right?"

Maria Mercurial meteored into public view in 2048, with the release of her hit single, "Who Weeps For The Children?"

Dumping Scandal Rocks Troubled Company

Perfekto Polymers was informed today that it is under investigation for an alleged violation of local toxic-waste disposal laws. Reliable sources in the City Council have informed this network that the documentation is "damning." If the council finds against Perfekto, the firm could face penalties ranging from heavy fines to loss of its operating permit in the Seattle city-state. The Salish-Shidhe Council has already filed a formal protest that such dumping violates numerous agreements between its government and the city.

This is the second major blow to Perfekto Polymers in 24 hours. Only yesterday, Perfekto CEO Andrew Masterson was found dead in his luxurious home on Queen Anne Hill, apparently the victim of a heart attack. The company's general manager for the Seattle region, Miguel Allende, was unavailable for comment. His office reports that he is attending "a special managerial briefing" in parent corporation Aztechnology's headquarters. At present, there is no date set for his return.

If Maria is re-addicted to dreamchips, give the players Item #2 from the news-nets.

Rocker Queen In BTL Scandal

According to reliable sources, Maria Mercurial, novahot rock singer, was admitted to a clinic at an undisclosed location today for treatment after a bad reaction to dreamchip abuse. Long the subject of speculation in the music industry, it appears that Mercurial's rumored addiction to BTL chips finally took its toll.

The Seattle branch of the Citizens for a Decent Society Policlub announced an immediate inquiry into the behavior of public performers. In a statement released just hours ago, CFDS chairwoman Margot Tipper says, "Do we really want such people as role models for our children? Taking drugs, burning BTLs, living lascivious lifestyles while they preach the overthrow of our great culture in their nefarious music: what kind of decent woman does things like that?"

Mercurial reached star status with the release of her hit single, "Who Weeps For The Children?" in 2048.

Star And Manager In Reconciliation—And Then Some!

Rocker star Maria Mercurial today canceled several scheduled appearances. The cancellation notice was issued by promoter Armando Hernandez. Until recently, the news in the music industry was that Ms. Mercurial had dumped Hernandez, and was being represented by rock impresario Max Foley. Notification was received yesterday at Musician's Guild Local 14 that Ms. Mercurial had, in fact, reinstated her contract with Hernandez.

Max Foley could not be reached for comment.

While Mercurial fans expressed disappointment at the news, despite full refunds offered on all tickets purchased so far, a number of those interviewed admitted that the reason for the cancellation satisfied even the most demanding concertgoer.

In a later press release, Mercurial and Hernandez announced their marriage, which took place at 0900 this morning, in a simple ceremony at City Hall. According to Maria: "We need some time to be by ourselves. Concerts, tours, and other such things can be so exhausting. We have been given a precious gift. We want time together to appreciate it. Our thanks go to everyone for their understanding, and especially to those who helped us most. *Gracias*." Who can argue with that?

Maria Mercurial achieved stardom almost overnight in 2048, with the release of her hit song, "Who Weeps For The Children?"

MARIA
MERCURIAL
IN CONCERT
IN CONCERT
IN CONCERT
IN CONCERT
IN CONCERT
MAY 23

Dreamchips

In the year 2050, drug use has largely been replaced by the use of illegally modified simsense chips. Technically, they generate simsense signals at amplitudes that intensify the experience to the limits of tolerance, or beyond. Common names for these are dreamchips, Better-Than-Life (BTL), and brain-strain, among others. Users are dreamchippers, deckheads, ROM-burners, and so on.

Dreamchips can induce numerous pre-programmed fantasies, with direct stimulation of the pleasure centers of the brain. They are profoundly addictive psychologically, though there is no evidence of physical addiction. The typical chip is timed to prevent undue trauma to nerve cells, and usually designed to burn itself out after one play to keep addicts coming back for more. Dreamchips plug into a standard datajack.

The constant use of dreamchips is highly addictive. In addition, extended use results in cumulative damage to brain cells, making the addict less sensitive to the effect. Thus, users must obtain more frequent doses or increase the amplitude of the signal still further, thus increasing brain cell damage. This vicious cycle usually ends with the death of the user. Other effects can be nerve damage, memory loss, or psychotic episodes.

Chips are often modified to play continuously. Timers, self-erase features, and similar safeguards can be overcome by technically competent persons. On the street, such modified chips are known as dreamgates. They are usually one-way gates. Subjects hooked into a continuous high-amplitude simsense broadcast suffer death within a short time as autonomic systems break down under the high-energy brain stimulation. Death by this means, either as suicide or as murder by giving someone a "loaded" chip, is a staple in cheap adventure fiction.

Dreamchips can be custom-designed, attuned to an individual's neural structure and psychological profile. Such chips can be addictive after one exposure. Withdrawal from a custom chip is agonizing, and users often expose themselves to high dosages of standard dreamchips if cut off from a custom chip.